Brands, Bandwagons & Bullshit

Collated advice & cautionary
tales for those embarking
on a career in marketing

HARRY LANG

For C & T

ISBN - 9798763938777

Thank You...

This book is a much better version of itself because I had significant help and input from a number of extremely bright people.

On the contributor side, many of the channel marketing segments were honed with implicit advice from the following group of marketing, communications and executive search professionals, to whom I owe a very decent and lengthy lunch: -

- Lisa Peacock Edwards, Senior Partner, Modern Executive Solutions
- Matt Kowaleczko, co-founder, Blue Machina
- Jamie Elliott, CEO, The Gate
- Jo Carr, Co-Founder and Chief Client Officer, Hope&Glory PR
- Nicole Goodwin – Marketing Director, Big Drop Brew Company
- Guy Wootton, Director of Business at Moy Park
- Dave Gilbert, Global Gaming Lead, Facebook.com
- Paddy Moogan, Founder, Aira.net
- Carrie Rose, Founder, Rise at Seven
- Ian Sims, founder of Rightlander.com

On the proofing side, thanks to Tones and Crawford plus Jazmin Hill, my colleague at Buzz Bingo, who spotted mistakes from a distance and honed my clunky phrasing into something resembling efficient copy.

Also, some praise should go to the UK Covid Lockdown, without which this book would never have been completed.

Finally, huge thanks and love to my family – Ma & Pa, The Lees, J & L, M.I.L. Ann, T & C – one day I'll publish one of these properly...

Preface

Why you shouldn't trust me

I fell into my marketing career, not through active choice, but rather a process of rapid and necessary elimination.

1997, 4am, somewhere in Newcastle. I'd shambled back from night out, sat down and written a list – all the careers that I might potentially explore as a graduate.

An hour later my list of 'lawyer', 'banker', 'hotelier', 'town planner' and the rest were scribbled then aggressively dismissed in red biro. Only one line remained – circled in green marker with a cigarette burn next to it:

'Marketing / advertising?'

I had no real clue what either entailed, to be honest. These days, advertising would at least conjure up images of Mad Men but back then, my only impression was that these were two careers in which I could perhaps retain some playful creativity whilst doing a proper commercial job that would eventually pay the bills. That, and advertising agencies apparently held fabulous parties.

Unfortunately, by the time I'd asked a favour from a friend's well connected father and been granted two weeks' work experience at Saatchi & Saatchi, it became clear I'd missed the bandwagon by at least a couple of years. While I could still smoke at my desk and the creative floor standardly took their lunch over the road in liquid form, the free sports cars and cocaine-fuelled pitch days were long gone. Advertising was a proper big business, and we were expected to treat it as such.

I converted my work experience into a runner's up spot on the graduate scheme at M&C Saatchi where I decided (via an extraordinary day hosting the Jordan F1 pit girls at Silverstone for Benson & Hedges) that I didn't want to be just an ad man (or a sponsorship host). I could see other channels - new, connected, exciting disciplines – the emergence of the digital age – and I wanted a piece.

In those days it was called consultancy – a bit of everything, depending on who paid and what the client was after. Now it's known as 'integrated marketing' – the ability to view all channels and disciplines as a collective supermarket in which you shop for items depending on your (or your client's) needs. It's the ideal career for anyone with a deficit of attention and the easily bored. Nothing's ever the same, everything changes – it's an imperfect world of opportunity, puppeteering, creativity, innovation, and risk.

For the last twenty-one years I've lived in this imperfect world – and for the most part enjoyed myself. So within this book I've tried to explain (to my understanding at least) what marketing is, what it can do, how you can become a better marketer and the ways in which everything can be clicked together like a Lego set so the sum becomes greater than the parts.

It's a subjective take, which means it's woefully incomplete – but it should start you thinking in some interesting directions.

The marketing environment is as different today from the start of my career as fashion is to the 1960s or music from the 1800s. As with technology, the marketing industry is in a constant, frequent, scary, and ill-defined state of movement, evolution, and flux. Every new idea, industry, platform, or technology becomes a bandwagon onto which hungry hoards try and attach themselves for personal gain.

It's a godawful mess - but a wonderful mess where bursts of genius occasionally bubble through seas of bullshit. Most people will sell you the earth, and even more have no clue what they're doing. This is why you shouldn't trust me – or anyone else – tomorrow's perfect marketing ideas haven't even been dreamt up yet and each day's a blank slate.

Whichever area of business you work in, marketing isn't going anywhere soon so it's worth understanding, at least at a conversational level. It's the petrol that drives the sales car – and without sales, even the most disruptive entity is going to come to a shuddering halt.

Hopefully this book will give you some ideas about how to break into the industry, the state 'marketing' is in today and the potential it has to educate, entertain and cajole change in the minds of the masses. Whilst I can't promise you results; I hope it will help you become a better marketer in the long run.

And to become more astute at identifying the bullshit and the bandwagons.

Contents

Preface 7

Introduction 15

Glossary 21

Part 1 – Getting Started 45

Chapter 1 47

What is Marketing? 47

Chapter 2 53

Breaking into Marketing & Advertising 53

Chapter 3 67

Marketing Channels 67

How to use data in Marketing? 69

How not to use data? 70

Chapter 4 97

A letter to my younger self - the advice I wish I'd had 97

Chapter 5 107

Why should you choose a career in marketing or advertising? . 107

Chapter 6 115

From shock to acceptance, get familiar with the 7 stages of job hunting 115

Chapter 7 121

Truth Bombs – Some Brief Suggestions on how not to delude yourself 121

Chapter 8 129

Getting A Job 129

Chapter 9...135

Let's Get Pivotal..135

Chapter 10 141

How to Write a Marketing Strategy 141

Chapter 11 149

What's the BIG Idea? 149

Chapter 12 153

Starting out on your Own 153

Part 2 – The Marketing Bit 157

Chapter 13 159

Chapter 14 165

Anticipation is the way to keep customers coming back for more

Chapter 15 173

Did you do that on purpose?..173

Chapter 16 181

Sometimes, marketing isn't the right thing to do..............181

Chapter 17 187

Don't hate the player. Hate the game.............................187

Chapter 18 193

What's love got to do with it? 193

Chapter 19 201

What marketers can learn from Skoda and Japanese rugby.....201

Chapter 20 207

The pros and cons of hitching your brand to an influencer.........207

Chapter 21 213

Rise of the Infants 213

Chapter 22 221

Creative awards remind brands of the need to take risks 221

Chapter 23 227

Making the most of Industry Conferences - An A to Z Guide 227

Chapter 24 233

The balance of good vs. evil 233

Why Amazon's success proves consumers are choosing easy over ethical 233

Chapter 25 239

Let's get ready to rumble 239

Everything wrong with the £100 million Brexit ad campaign 239

Chapter 26 245

Generation A to Zzzz... 245

How to communicate with teenagers without boring them to death

Chapter 27 251

When Marketing Piggybacks on Sport..................................... 251

Chapter 28 257

Is this really the best a man can get? 257

Chapter 29 261

Ho, Ho, Woe.. 261

Sometimes they get it right... 261

Chapter 30 269

New tech for old problems and how to keep up with the disruptors

Chapter 31 277

Playing the Game 277

In football, as in marketing, you ignore the rules at your peril..... 277

Chapter 32 281

Hubble, Bubble, Toil & Trouble 281

Chapter 33 289

The game of life and how commerce is influenced by play 289

Chapter 34 295

You can't ditch brand for performance marketing – even in
digital

Chapter 35 301

The dark side of the moon 301

Chapter 36 311

It's the beginning of the end of the travel industry's golden age
.... 311

Chapter 37 317

What if God was one of us? 317

Epilogue.. 323

Introduction

"If you can see the bandwagon, you've probably missed it"

Sage advice from my first boss many, many years ago that I recall every time I get wind of any new, exciting money-making opportunity.

In marketing, it's easy to get caught up in the hype – the latest channel, brand, agency, or media outlet. Cutting the useful from the useless is a constant battle.

It's similar when you're picking a career. Marketing, Advertising, PR, and Media are all inherently designed to sound awesome, but how can you possibly know which path is right for you without getting stuck in? You won't know the facts until it's too late – so the best thing to do is research what's out there and make the most informed decisions possible.

I've listened to a lot of people in the marketing industry – experts, clients, agencies, and colleagues. Sometimes their words are incredibly insightful, but just as frequently, they're utter bullshit. This business is a cornucopia of errant geniuses and wonderful charlatans – each of whom is trying to sell something.

Occasionally, somewhere in the middle, there are words that shudder true in their frankness - such as my favorite assessment of a tricky working day in my first big agency:

"Today can take it's arse and go fuck itself".

In that instance, back in the early 2000s, the agency was 141, part of Bates, subsequently hoovered up by the behemoth that is WPP. That's just the way it is – the marketing industry is amazing – but like any industry, it can't half suck, too.

Should you choose to start your career on the agency side, it's likely you'll have a few days that warrant a similar battle cry. But don't assume by comparison that working in-house on the client side of the fence is a floriferous utopia. It can be equally hellish in its own political, slow, meandering, bureaucratic, nonsensical way - that's marketing.

As a discipline and an industry, the very things that make it great are also its biggest frailties. And that leads to one core truism:

Marketing is never perfect.

How could it be? Every second of every day, everything that helps inform your decisions changes. Trends disperse, media pivots, demographics shift, geographies imbalance, economies peak and trough, products fail, creative is subjective, Pandemics arrive and strategy's a Rubik's Cube of a conundrum. With no binary right/ wrong to reassure you, it's unsurprising how many ill-educated folks in other professions are self-proclaimed marketing geniuses.

Creative, strategy and tactics are all subjective until proven to work, so owning your knowledge and defending your informed position against compromised, beige outputs is something you'll have to become a Jedi in.

And then you get to the customers…

The general public hasn't evolved to respond to your campaigns. Most consumers, given the choice, would never see an ad, poster, digital banner, social post, direct mail piece or SMS message from a brand ever again. Your task, whether as strategist, creative, copywriter, suit, planner, buyer, or client is to make people aware of your brand, persuade them that it can be trusted and is better than all competitors, and convince them the price is right and to hand over their hard-earned cash. Sometimes, you need to do all this on a piece of digital real estate no bigger than a stamp.

It's not easy.

Therein lies the joy. You'll never work the same day twice, the people tend to be sparkly, creative, intelligent, and bonkers in equal measure and you'll constantly be challenged to find impossible answers in zero time.

Imagination, thick skin, and a grafting work ethic aren't just nice to haves – they're bottom rung essentials.

If you want predictable, be an accountant. Work in insurance. Gel your hair and wear pointy shoes as you show busloads of monied tossers around unaffordable houses in real estate. Just don't pick a marketing career.

If you're still reading, excellent. You've got the stones to see challenges as opportunities and the above sounds interesting rather than terrifying. This game just might be for you.

But hold fire – for any Mad Men aficionados out there, it isn't all Scotch, sports cars and expense accounts. Those days died out in the early '90s.

Marketing, whilst in one of the higher paying career brackets, isn't a route to instant richness. It's a passion project in the early years that gets progressively more rewarding as you climb the greasy pole (see Chapter 2 for more on this).

This book is designed to help anyone considering or starting out in a marketing career – as well as seasoned pros in other departments who are flummoxed by jargon and fed up with being made to feel stupid by their CMO. Built in part using notes and tips I've found valuable myself, it also contains snippets from a number of industry experts plus segments from articles I've written for Marketing Week and Campaign. The topics are wide-ranging, broaching channel marketing tactics, brand strategy and some of the pitfalls you'll encounter on your own journey.

'Part 1: Getting Started' covers the foundations - things you might want to consider before you get your first job whilst 'Part 2 – The Marketing Bit' branches out into the strategy, tactics, and campaigns that brands employ to give them an edge (or sometimes get very, very wrong).

This isn't a 'self-help' book, nor does it profess to hold all the answers. Think of it less as a Sat Nav directing you to your perfect marketing career and more like a shopping list to browse. The baking of the cake is totally up to you, but hopefully you'll pick up some useful ideas, directions, and suggestions for ingredients over the coming pages. This book is purposefully simplistic to better serve as an introduction to marketing, advertising, PR and media. There are plenty of further reading titles out there - many of which promise the earth and are full of speculative nonsense, so shop carefully.

If you have any questions or you're stuck in a rut, please do get in touch – you can reach me via Linked In or Twitter @MrHarryLang.

I hope you enjoy the book and best of luck!

Harry

Glossary

Yep, you'd usually expect to see this at the back of the book, next to picture credits, attributions, and some other guff. But in this book, it made much more sense to run through some of the terminology, channels, and B.S. that you'll likely come across in an agency or client-side career sooner rather than later.

Term	Proper Description	TL;DR
A/B Testing	Testing two versions of a webpage, email, landing page, CTA, advert etc. to see which one performs best. Then you go with that one until you test new variants	"What version's better, design A or B? B? Let's go with that" That's A/B testing.
Acquisition Marketing	Using digital media to acquire new customers – usually led by PPC, Display, Paid Social, SEO, DRTV & ASO	Using digital media to find and convert customers
Advertising	Displaying a product or service on a paid media channel in order to sell more of said product. According to Bob Hoffman, the purpose of advertising is to make a brand famous. I agree.	Anything you have to pay for that's designed to sell something

Affiliate Marketing	A media channel whereby you deal with a website owner or network to buy traffic from their sites. Deals tend to be CPA (Cost Per Acquisition – e.g., £20 per customer) Revenue Share (they take a % of each customers future spend with you) or Hybrid, which is a bit of both	It's frustrating how rich some affiliates get, but if they're good, it's a highly accountable acquisition channel
Analytics	Using data and data analysis to interpret patterns of behaviour and gain insights about your customer, product, website, or campaign so you can do it better next time	The use of data to make better decisions. A good analyst will make you look better
Application Programming Interface (API)	Rules in computer programming allowing an application ('Apps') to take information from a service and use it in either their own application or in data analysis	A way for computers to talk to each other – a data Walkie Talkie
App Store Optimisation (ASO)	Like SEO (See below) the way in which you position and frame your App in IOS or Android stores, so it indexes higher than competitors in	Look in the App Store. Apps at the top are good at this (but fake reviews help. A lot.)

	search rankings. A wonderful channel if you can get it right.	
Above the Line (ATL)	Channels that deploy advertising to a wider target audience, e.g. television (TVC), radio, or billboards. Below the Line (BTL) is targeted, e.g. Digital Ads, Paid Social, CRM	Old days, ATL was trendy. Now BTL is level par
Artificial Intelligence (A.I.)	A system or process that replicates human intelligence. AI programs can demonstrate image perception, reasoning, and voice recognition.	The cause of – and answer to – all of a marketer's future problems
Attribution Modelling	Rules that determine how much credit for sales should be assigned to touchpoints or channels in the acquisition journey (so, a customer sees an ad, looks up the product on line then researches more on an affiliate site before clicking to access the website – each channel is credited a % giving a full picture of their value)	"I'd like to thank display, PPC and TV for contributing to this sale…" Read the long version. It's important.
Augmented Reality	Also known as 'immersive technologies', whilst virtual reality displays 100% digitally	What you see when a real image/ video is

	created worlds, augmented merges the real with the digital. Used to great effect to show makeup, furniture and paint in real life examples, the potential applications are only just warming up	overlaid with cool digital content to create a richer experience
Business to Business (B2B)	Marketing one brand to other businesses (related to 'Software as a Service' or the SaaS industry	The less glamourous (but often better paid) version of B2C marketing
Business to Consumer (B2C)	Marketing towards the general public (consumers)	The more glamourous (thus worse paid) version of B2B marketing
Brand	A product manufactured by a particular company under a particular name. Originating from the 'brand' burned onto cows to show who owns it.	How a product or company is perceived by those who experience it
Brand Architecture	The structure by which a brand (or brand family) is constructed. A Branded House (like Virgin) shares a common name while a House of Brands (like Unilever) has lots of different brand names under one roof	A pyramid with the master brand name at the top

Bounce Rate	The % of website visitors who land on your site, don't like it then leave without doing anything you wanted them to do	It's good, but it's not the one
Brand Advertising	Building a brand's profile, awareness and equity through big budget ethereal campaigns that suggest a lot of warm wooly things but don't try and push you into buying the product. (That's done by the other media channels)	Big ad campaigns, normally on TV – good ones make you go 'wow'
Chat Bots	AI-based technology that employs instant messaging to chat with customers and site visitors in real time, saving cost on real people and employing algorithms to drive desired behaviours	Computer says: "How are you today? Can I interest you in a 4 year warranty?"
Churn	A % given to the volume of customers who leave a website or stop buying a certain product or service	When a customer decides they've had enough
Click Bait	Teasing headline copy on ads that drive naïve users to click them. The sea cucumber of the online media world. Tends	Mail Online is king of this space. Nuff said.

	to start something like: "You'll never believe XX happened".	
Click Through Rate (CTR)	The number of clicks digital customers make as a % of the total number of actions they could have taken from a banner ad or web page	The % of clicks a digital asset generate
Content Management System (CMS)	The program which allows you to manage all aspects of content on a website	The simple back office for most websites. The complex back office is usually in some format of code.
Conversational Marketing	Moving buyers through sales funnels by utilising 'one at a time' questions, like a real time conversation thus enhancing the user experience through a feedback model that drives higher engagement and greater loyalty	Humanising sales messages increases the chances you'll get a positive result
Conversion Rate Optimisation (CRO)	Using analysis to improve the % of people who make it from first click through registration to becoming a paying customer on a website	Making first click to purchase more efficient
Copy	Best described by fabled Ad man Derek Walker: "Copy is a	Weaponised words.

	message that supports, proclaims and defends an idea that a piece of advertising puts forth".	
Copywriting	A posh word used by advertising agencies for writing ads. You can guess what 'Copy Checking' means.	Literally writing with a purpose and objective in mind
Customer Relationship Management (CRM)	How you keep all your customer communications under one roof, often with one software platform. Connected to your database your CRM strategy defines how, what and when you communicate certain messages to your customers	The closest thing your brand will have to a friendship with customers (if done well)
Cost Per Acquisition	How much you're willing to spend on digital marketing to get one new depositing/ paying customer. (Relates to your CPA and conversion capabilities)	How much for a new customer?
Cost Per Click	How much you have to bid/ spend in a digital media channel such as PPC with Google AdWords to get one click	How much for a curtain twitcher?

Call to Action (CTA)	It's really very important to tell people what you want them to do at the end of any campaign. Click Here/ Search Now/ Visit Us/ Sniff This – whatever media, a strong CTA is the cherry on top of a good campaign.	Buy Now!
Demographics	How to profile your customers – multiple metrics are available but age, sex, location are the most common	Who/ What/ Where
Design	The process by which concepts are translated into visual assets. Art Directors in agencies look after the visual concept while Copywriters hone the idea and words. Designers then turn the messy concept into commercially successful art	The team that makes ideas look pretty
Direct Mail (DM)	Marketing assets you send to targeted customers in the post – everything from postcards to luxury hampers come under the auspices of DM)	Posted campaigns

Direct Response TV (DRTV)	TV advertising that aggressively pushes a Call to Action (as opposed to Brand Advertising). Cheaper than brand ads for both production and media.	TV ads selling something fast.
Direct to Consumer (D2C)	Fed up with Amazon taking a slice from all your profits? Then cut them and all other distributors out of the loop by selling direct to customers. Dyson is a successful exponent of this and is big enough to get away with it without ostracizing its retail partners.	Create product, advertise product, get consumer to buy via your website directly. That's it.
Display Advertising	Digital Ads that are image led (as opposed to text-led PPC ads). You can buy these through AdWords, network deals with media owners or directly with affiliates	Those banners on the side of websites you tend not to click.
Econometrics	"The quantitative analysis of economic phenomena based on the concurrent development of theory and observation related by appropriate methods of inference". Nope, me neither.	Using maths to model current and future events

Engagement	Your ability to communicate with and form a relationship with your target and current customers so they're invested in your brand	You online? You like what you see? You're being engaged!
Forecast	Defining what you believe to be the KPI and financial outcomes of your marketing activity – vital for budget management (and for getting hold of budget in the first place)	Predicting how much it costs and how much it delivers
General Data Protection Regulation (GDPR)	A regulation in EU law that covers data protection and privacy. Adhering to GDPR rules protects the general public's data and stops companies from acting irresponsibly in how and what it sends to customers	When people opt out of communications, GDPR means companies think twice about emailing them
Geo Fencing	Creepy as it sounds, targeting consumers with specific messages depending on where they are is commonplace already. Think of Waze showing a push notification as you approach a petrol station. We're at the tip of the iceberg in geo targeting	"You hungry? Burger King is 2 minutes that way". And repeat.

H1 Tag	An HTML tag used to identify the highest level of information on a page. H1s play an important role in search engine optimization (SEO) and make it easier to index content. If something is in an H1 tag, Google knows it's important.	How you tag a web page's title
Influencer Marketing	Using vapid humanized airsocks* with strong social media followings to share your campaign message. Sometimes a necessary evil. (see Chapter 9 – 'Love Island') *Not all of them	A necessary evil for some brands targeting younger audiences.
Integrated Marketing	The Swiss Army knife of strategy – pull out the right tool for the job, except magically you can use lots of them together and they work seamlessly	Like an orchestra of channels playing together in harmony
Interactive Content	360 degree videos for estate agents, augmented reality ads, ads that engage as they sell. Interactive ads make people feel more connected to brands and more involved in the buying process	Allowing buyers to engage with (thus feel closer to) a digital advert

Internet of Things (IOT)	The network of objects that include sensors and software allowing them to exchange data with other devices and systems over the Internet (e.g. your car booking its own service)	"The fridge is now sentient. I, for one, welcome our new refrigerated overlords"
JavaScript	A coding language that works with HTML to make dynamic web page content. Contact forms, sign-in pages and shopping carts are all the children of JavaScript	Can you code? If you could, you may use Java
Key Performance Indicators (KPIs)	Metrics that you define as targets when you set your strategy and before you launch any campaign. Could be CPA £, Conversion %, Total Revenue, or bums on seats	How to set objectives and targets.
Last-click attribution	All the 'credit' goes to the customer's last digital touchpoint before converting, not factoring other previous channel engagements. You're only seeing part of the story, meaning you'll ignore potentially valuable channels	Last channel standing wins the prize

	in the future (See U-Shaped Attribution)	
Lead	A person or company that has shown even the slightest interest in your brand. More prevalent in B2B marketing	A new contact.
Lead Generation	How you go about generating more leads – usually through rich content, campaign activity, partnerships, and referrals	Attracting new contacts
Lifetime Value (LTV)	How much a customer is worth to you before they Churn. Their LTV minus their CPA with give your total Net revenue amount	How much a customer is worth in total
Marketing Automation	Software that enables you to automate marketing processes thus saving you time and money (Doesn't always work - See 'Programmatic').	Robots do your job
Market Research	Quantitative research dealing with numbers and statistics, while qualitative	What it says on the tin.

	research deals with words and meanings.	
Narrowcasting	Sending a media message to a highly targeted audience, such as email CRM	The opposite of Broadcasting
Net Promoter Score (NPS)	The likelihood that someone would recommend your company to other people on a 1–10 scale.	A feedback scoring system or popularity device
Neuromarketing	Using physiological and neural signals to deliver insights into customer motivations, preferences, and decisions, thus informing advertising, product development and pricing to achieve an optimised response	Analysing brain activity and nervous systems? Yep, this is bound to end well…
Omnichannel Marketing	Lots of channels working together at the same time towards a common goal so the sum is greater than the individual parts	The modern description of 'Integrated Marketing' (see above)
Organic Search	Natural and unpaid results users receive after questioning a search engine, which then crawl web pages and rank content for relevance.	SEO helps your website position higher in natural search

Optimisation	Analysing the performance of a channel or campaign, noting how it works/ doesn't work and making it deliver more in its next iteration	Making any channel or campaign work better
Pay Per Click (PPC)	Bidding on keywords on search engines. Popular keywords cost more, and prices vary day to day. Longtail Keywords are phrases, so attract less search volume but are often more closely targeted and cheaper	Those text ads at the top of a Google search
Personalisation	Giving your customers a more personalised experience that will likely convert better by creating marketing materials that appeal to specific groups.	Creating for the individual, not the group
Privacy Marketing	With fines in the hundreds of millions being handed out you need to play by the rules when it comes to communicating with customers and using their personal data. Effectively, it'll take more work as you have to 'earn' the right to speak with your targets.	GDPR is the tip of the privacy iceberg. Understand the rules and stick to them like glue or pay the price

Product Marketing	Bringing a product to market and ensuring that it sells. Requires bespoke strategy and campaign tactics often led by a Product Marketing team	A niche team that focusses on marketing one product
Programmatic Marketing	Using automation technology in buying and selling media – supposedly to increase efficiency and ROI but yet to be perfected and rumours of fraud are still rife. One day soon this will be how we plan and buy digital media though	Robots buy ads for you. Sometimes, you don't get defrauded
Public Relations (PR)	Managing the release of information to affect the public's perception of a brand. Could be a product launch, new hire, crisis management or campaign. Relates closely to social media and SEO.	Doing the work of journalists to make noise for your brand
Push Notifications	Pop ups that draw on browser behaviour to re-engage with customers by delivering a fitting message or CTA. Handy for CRMs in the ever more restrictive world of GDPR	Web messages used to target people who have shown interest but failed to convert

Quality Score	A Google Ads metric that rates how relevant your PPC ads and landing pages are to your chosen keywords. Your estimate is based on ad relevance to keywords, expected click-through rate (CTR) and landing page experience (inc. site performance)	Are your ads relevant? You'll do well then.
Quantum Computing	Quantum computers are able to theoretically work on millions of computations at once. Applications include mobile reach, A.I. and 'Quantum Annealing' (helping adverts find more people at lower cost)	Like A.I. on crack
Regulatory Bodies	There's a few you need to be aware of if you work in marketing, advertising, media, and PR. Here's the top line list:- The ASA – Advertising Standards Authority CAP - The UK Code of Non-broadcast Advertising and Direct & Promotional Marketing	They like to say 'no'.

	CMA – Competition and Markets Authority GDPR - General Data Protection Regulation Ofcom - The Office of Communications PRCA – Public Relations & Communications Association	
Retargeting	Serving ads for products or services that customers have viewed previously – on second glance, they're more likely to convert.	Showing an ad to the same customer more than once, often in a different channel
Return on Investment (ROI)	The cash you get back as revenue in exchange for the money you invested in marketing. You hope the former is greater than the latter	Buy a Lotto ticket. Win a Pound. Your ROI is 0%
Return on Advertising Spend (ROAS)	As per ROI, a measure of what you get back as a % of the money you spent on a campaign	Like ROI but just for ad spend
Sales	Chicken and egg as to whether marketing supports the sales team or sales is a function of marketing. It's an irrelevant debate as both rely on each other for success	Those who sell products directly to customers

Search Engine Optimisation (SEO)	Using website quality, keywords, and offsite link building/ online PR to build the profile of your site so it goes up the page rankings in Google (other search engines are available. But not relevant)	Relatively cheap, potentially great for volume – takes time, effort, and skill to get right. Pick a good agency.
Shoppable Posts	Instagram leads the market but other networks are catching up the ability to buy what you see in influencer posts	A fool & their money…
Social Media	'Organic Social' is communicating with the public via your brand's social pages. Paid Social is when you buy ads on the social network	Twitter etc. – posts & ads
Social Messaging Apps	Messenger, WeChat, WhatsApp – 55 billion messages a day are sent on the latter. Customers use these channels to communicate, brands are following suit	A new and hitherto untapped channel – a minefield of potential annoyance
Social Proof	A psychological phenomenon in which people seek direction from those around them to	How the weak-willed and weaker-minded are misled on social media

	determine how they are supposed to act or think in any given situation.	
Software as a Service (SaaS)	Software that is hosted by another company, which stores your information in the cloud for example HubSpot and Salesforce	SaaS Marketing used to be lower paid, niche B2B. Not anymore.
Spam	Unwanted or unsolicited digital communications (often an email or SMS) that gets sent out in bulk arbitrarily in the hope of catching the tiny % of people naïve enough to believe its contents	Not the tinned meat (but just as unpalatable)
Sponsorship	A brand-building channel that weds a brand to a property (sports team/ TV show etc.) to build brand awareness and leverage shared emotional attachment	Paying to be associated with something with high visibility in the public consciousness
Strategy	The long-term game plan of any business. In marketing terms it's the cookery book you design showing how and when ingredients are added to make the perfect cake	Tactics help you win a battle. Strategy will win the war

Streaming	Listening to music or watching video in 'real time', instead of downloading a file to your computer	Big with Twitch for esports shoutcasters
TV Advertising	The daddy of brand building channels. Expensive to make ads, expensive to plan and buy the media but the home of every great integrated campaign	Making the ads you see on the box
Unique Selling Proposition (USP)	The core of any marketing strategy – what it is that your brand can do that no other can. Your essence.	The one thing that differentiates what you're selling
User Experience (UX)	The way in which your customers interact with your business online – most commonly relates to usability and ease of navigation around websites	How you intuitively flow around a website
User Generated Content (UGC)	The global behemoth that is social media (and the ensuing gas cloud of influencers that floats in its wake) has built UGC as a huge marketing channel. If you can induce the public, especially highly followed individuals, to display your brand in a rich context the	Bloody brilliant – get customers to build your campaigns for you. Relevant by definition.

	brand gets a natural validation	
User Interface (UI)	The graphical layout of an application or website (inc. button, image and copy layout). Closely correlated with UX to define and improve overall usability of a site	The things you see and respond to on a website
U-Shaped Attribution	A typical u-shaped model would award 40% of the new FTD acquisition to the first channel aa customer interacts with and another 40% to the last, with 20% split evenly between any intermediary channels.	Giving credit where credit's due to digital channels
Viral Media	A campaign that is so good, engaging, or funny that it spreads from peer to peer virally, like a cold. Memes, snippet videos and branded Tweets (good ones) sit in this bucket	A funny WhatsApp video – but monetized
Vision Statement	A concise summary of where your brand is going in the future (if things go well). Similar to a brand mission, it sits next to brand positioning,	"I have a dream." No, that's a vision.

	personality, voice, and values in a Brand Guidelines.	
Visual Search	Google & Pinterest's Lens products make your phone's camera a search tab. Click & search everything from barcodes to historical buildings, intuitive search's next phase is here	Page 1 of 'The Stalker's Manifesto'
Voice Search	Alexa, Siri, Assistant etc. – over 50% of searches are already voice activated. The genius of getting a bug into everyone's houses was when Big Tech developed smart speakers – had they given them away, there would've been uproar	"Why is Google showing me ads for hemorrhoid cream? Oh…"
Word of Mouth	A channel whereby customers tell their peers about a product or service. Amazing if you can manage it due to the P2P trust factor, but incredibly hard to plan for.	Gossip benefitting a brand
YouTube	The UK's second biggest search engine. Great for highlight viewing, but also the cause of so many Streamers and Shoutcasters earning a living as 'Influencers'	Owned by the world's biggest search engine.

Part 1 – Getting Started

The first half of Brands, Bandwagons & Bullshit covers the foundations of strategy, channel marketing and the things you need to know before applying for your first job and planning your career in the creative industries.

Chapter 1

What Is Marketing?

"In the real world, consumers are massively not joining "conversations" about your brand. Not committed to having a "relationship" with it. They do not want to "engage with your content," and are not fascinated by your "brand stories." They do not consider themselves part of a "community" or "tribe" that has your brand at the centre".

Bob Hoffman, 2021

Wise words from the living legend of marketing that is Mr. Hoffman, rubbishing much of the BS floated around the industry like a pervading cloud of holistic piffle. And largely true – nobody really cares. So what the hell does 'marketing' do, anyway?

If you already work in the creative media industries (let's umbrella those as design, advertising, marketing, digital, social, media, SEO, content, CRM, and PR for the sake of neatness) then chances are, you've heard the spiel numerous times in various guises during your background research, interviews, workshops, TED Talks, on YouTube and at conferences. If you're new to this world, well here it is.

We'll take the traditional route of plagiarism first as in this instance, the definition from The Chartered Institute of Marketing in 2007 sounds credible, if a little matronly:-

"Marketing is the activity, set of institutions and processes for creating, communicating, delivering, and exchanging offerings that have value for customers, clients, partners, and society at large".

So far so good, right? Kind of? Nearly?

Nope.

To the uneducated eye, it's still as clear as a political press release. Lesson 1 – marketing is about selling and misdirection. Often very well executed and always with an objective to achieve value for the product owner that exceeds the value to the consumer whilst coming at a minimal cost to the product owner and the highest achievable cost to the consumer.

Still not clear? No, me neither. So here's a mini breakdown of the steps involved in a generic marketing process: -

1)   Creating products that are perceived as being (much) more valuable than the sum of their parts – this is where a strong brand earns its keep

2)   Inducing people to want to buy said product for (much) more than it costs to make – this can be through marketing campaigns or direct sales and is often known as acquisition. Hell will freeze over before anyone agrees whether marketing is a function of sales or vice versa but turning them from a curious lead into a paying customer is often called conversion.

3)   Keeping your customers engaged and happy through after sales care, new and improved product quality and heart-warming relationship building communications and after sales care. This is known as retention.

4)   Minimising the loss of returning customers. It's cheaper to keep a customer than it is to find a new one, so a good marketing strategy always tends and nurtures its loyal base. Sometimes, these customers simply don't come back. So you do everything in your power to change their minds – this is reactivation.

I always find these kinds of multi-faceted concepts are best delivered through an analogy, so here's what integrated channel Marketing looks like in its most naked form:-

1)   Imagine you're a farmer and one day you drop some corn in the fire and it pops – congratulations - you've invented popcorn

2)   You name your tasty invention 'Fabulous Popping Corn' (or 'FPC' hereafter) and sell it in bright red boxes with a corn stalk on the front being struck by lightning – this is branding

3)   You build a website and a suite of digital assets and start selling FPC online – this is where design, UX and UI (see Glossary) comes in

4)   You add a bunch of keywords to your website like 'Best sugary snack', so people find you more easily through Google and other search engines – this is Search Engine Optimisation (SEO – see Glossary)

5)   You decide you want to sell more volume, so you bid on the term 'Sweet snacks' in Google AdWords – this is Pay Per Click or PPC.

6)   A year in and you want to understand and communicate with your customer base more effectively, so you email customers who have purchased in over 3 months with a 'buy one, get one free' offer – this is Customer Relationship Management (CRM) pushing a Sales Promotion.

7)   To generate more brand awareness you put the FPC logo on the shirts of your local football team and write a press release about the deal. This is sponsorship promoted through PR and can also help SEO.

8)   With your new football fan base you push out stories and videos about the players enjoying your product on Twitter, Facebook, Instagram, and YouTube – you've kicked off your social media presence and activation.

9)   Year two sales are strong, and a big supermarket chain decides to stock FPC – you make a TV ad, a radio ad and buy print advertising and billboards in key cities – this is Above the Line advertising.

10)   You do a deal with Netflix – every time a person renews their subscription they get a free bag of FPC – this is a 3rd party partnership facilitating a new customer sampling campaign.

11)   You expand internationally – good for you! But Fabulous Popping Corn translates to 'Rubbish Crumb Farts' in simplified Chinese. Not cool. You naturally feel an urgent need to employ a localisation expert to trans-create your brand name, website, and marketing campaigns.

The thing is even bad marketing can have an impact. Try and remember the most annoying ads you've ever seen – the inane characters, teeth-grating soundtrack – probably the odd animated creature. A great proportion of those ads actually worked – they brought the brand to front of mind, generated noise, and interest and if the campaign ran for a while in several iterations, you could safely assume it sold some product, too.

"You miss 100 % of shots you don't take" Wayne Gretzky, 1983

This quote has been deployed in marketing meetings more often than a plate of stale biscuits, yet *some* marketing is (almost always) better than *no* marketing. Even the most abhorrent ad, email, branded video, or social post will have some kind of positive impact ('Go Compare' for yourself). Of course, a well-researched brief and astute media strategy will do better but it's a handy reminder that having something live is almost always better than being a silent wallflower.

Chapter 2

Breaking Into Marketing & Advertising

Decisions, decisions...

Choosing which marketing path to take is question number 1. There are numerous verticals, disciplines, and channels, but we'll make a start with one of the big early decisions – client side vs. agency.

Client Side

So, you want to get into a marketing department. Cool. It's not like you need specialist A Levels or a suite of science qualifications. The route in is a simple, if extremely competitive, funnel. Graduate schemes are easy enough to find on agency and client HR websites and, with a 2:1 degree or better from a reputable University you'll just be up against a few thousand other eager souls, bursting with ambition, brains, and bravado. It's tough, but the education and fluid career pathway you'll get in a Diageo, Unilever, Kraft, or Toyota graduate scheme is hard to beat and will set you up as a solid marketer for life.

Agency Account Management

As with client side the bigger agencies and networks have graduate schemes. Equally hard to get into, nowhere nearly as well organized, it's more a question of beating the other candidates to get your foot in the door. Once there, the strong survive, but IMHO there's no better training than the fast paced, multi-client, unhinged panic, and team camaraderie of a good agency. Whilst client side is more of a formal education, agency is school of life. It's up to you to grab opportunities, skills, and contacts off your own back but you'll learn more hard skills in year one than anywhere else.

If grad schemes are proving too exclusive for either Client side or Agency (90%+ of applicants won't get an offer, so seriously, don't beat yourself up about it!) then there are numerous other ways to maneuver yourself into consideration, some of which are covered in Chapter 3.

Copy & Art Direction

The traditional training pilgrimage for wannabe creatives was (and I believe still is) Tony Cullingham's Watford Advertising Course at West Herts College. With fifteen places available each year, it's very much not for everyone, so taking the direct path has worked for many hero creatives over the years. Obviously being all about spreading your creative wings, getting noticed is a chance to show what you're made of.

Back in the day, my favourite stories included the creative team painting their portfolio on the pavement outside a Creative Director's office. In the digital age, one clever applicant bid on the PPC keywords for the names of all the major Executive Creative Directors in London. Knowing they (like most people) might Google themselves once in a while the ECDs would be met with an intro letter and CV. That guy's conversion rate was, by all accounts, extraordinary.

Persistence, imagination, and luck are all needed in equal measure, unless of course you can rely on the Career Faerie – otherwise known as nepotism. It's alive and well and if you know anyone in the business, do everything in your power to persuade them to give you a shot. Rightly or wrongly, it's still the shortest path to success.

Do It Yourself

The digital age has taken off the shackles of the traditional career path. Anyone with a laptop can learn how to build a WordPress site in an afternoon and set up an affiliate business to monetise within a matter of days. Coding is a hobby, esports are a paid profession, music is sharable in a click, TikTok, Instagram and Snapchat monetises any old shite as long as it attracts eyeballs. All of these things require marketing skills – brand building, copywriting, customer communication, CRM, forecasting, conversion, retention, and reactivation – there really are no limits whatsoever, but a head start in how to find, nurture, and keep customers is guaranteed to make you better, faster if you go down the entrepreneurial path.

You know who's a brilliant brand marketer? Bloody Jordan. Katie Price builds audiences, generates reach, demands attention, moves with the times, reinvents her brand, achieves regular PR coverage and rakes in the Dollars like a squirrel hoards nuts. Maddening but nonetheless true.

Nailing an Interview

However you find out about a job in the industry, you can't avoid the dreaded interview.

That said, there's no reason you should dread it – flip it on its head and the interview process is a simple funnel. Lots of people apply, thus feeding into the top of the funnel and one name pops out of the bottom to claim the prize. That individual can attribute their success to a blend of factors, loosely (but not exclusively) made up from these traits:-

1. Education
2. Appropriate fit for the job
3. Experience
4. Enthusiasm
5. Emotional Intelligence
6. How well they prepared for the interview/s
7. Value they'll deliver to the business
8. Cost
9. Secret Sauce

Before you soil your draws in trepidation, here's something that'll make you feel a little less daunted: – the last seven of those nine things require no long term planning, expensive education nor nepotistic contacts and, as such, are entirely within your grasp if you approach the interview with the right research in hand and in the right mindset.

A Word from the Pros – Lisa Peacock Edwards, Senior Partner at Modern Executive Solutions

How to interview well

Be Prepared - it sounds obvious, but this is where most people go wrong. Research the company – their corporate website, social accounts, and people - to get a feel for their brands, who their customers are and who their competitors are. Also, research your interviewer - LinkedIn, Facebook, IG etc is a good start (just don't tell them about it in the interview!) Instead, see if you have any common interests and then highlight them in your answers.

Read the job description - you'll be surprised how many people don't and are easy to discount as a result. Think about what you've done that matches what they are looking for and practice answers around these things.

S.T.A.R - this is the Head-hunter's secret to answering all questions effectively. Think about your answer in terms of S - the situation, T - the task, A - the action taken and R - the result. This is all you need to consider in order to give the best reply in a concise and effective way.

Dress for Success - think about what your mum would say! Seriously, your interviewer is more likely to be closer to your mum's age than yours and will likely have the same lens on things. Even if your attire is casual, make sure that you locate your iron and hairbrush and use it.

The Handshake - it's important. Your dad told you so, and he was right. A strong handshake and eye contact when you first meet goes a long way. If it's a hot day or you're nervous, make sure your hands aren't sweaty before meeting your interviewer.

Act the Part - non-verbal communication is 80%+ of the conversation - so eye contact counts - likewise your posture. Above all, remember to smile - not like a lunatic but like the warm, relaxed, and confident person you are.

Don't play it too cool - the interviewer wants to know that you really want the job. Think about why you do and be able to explain it in two or three points.

Say 'Thank You' – sending a follow up note is very important - tell them why you're interested, use a couple of points that came up in the interview to emphasise how your experience fits the role and thank them for considering you.

How to interview badly

Watch your mouth - it sounds simple, but people really do judge if you come across as overly friendly or swear in your interview as it seems like you're not taking it seriously. If you do swear by accident, then be sure to apologise.

Be on time - There is no excuse for being late for an interview. I always get there super early and grab a coffee next door, so you're not flustered and then arrive at the venue ten mins early. (FYI arriving too early is also a no-no)

Don't talk too much - if you've answered a question in full then it's ok to stop talking. And remember to think before you answer - nobody minds a moment of silence in exchange for a well-crafted response

Education

In the majority of cases, your level of education is a tick box exercise. Yes, formal copy and art direction training are highly regarded if not essential creative stepping stones but for agency or client suits, a degree is a stick by which HR departments can easily grade long lists. For tier 1 client-side roles (Unilever, Coke, P&G etc) and top 20 agencies, a 2:1 degree is the smallest pond they'd ever need to go fishing in – they're spoiled for choice in such a popular market.

 If you came out with a lesser degree (or even better, no degree at all) congratulations! You've spared yourself a mercenary multi-stage interview process over several soul deflating days against more experienced candidates who probably interned at the firm and whose uncle is Chairman.

Fuck that.

Now you can go fishing in the much wider and more accessible pond which is the 25 million + active enterprises operating across Europe and 100 million + companies currently trading around the world.

Each and every one of them needs marketing talent in some guise, so don't limit yourself to the perceived 'premium' graduate schemes – you'll pick up an entirely new and pragmatic set of skills operating at the coal face of a start-up, anyway.

Appropriate fit for the job

Let's step into the interviewer's shoes for a second. They need to find the best person to do the job in question at the budget they've allocated (and had approved) for the role and within a timeframe that doesn't leave gaps in their ability to deliver.

Whether they're the HR business partner running first round phone interviews, the manager to whom the role reports or the boss who likes to sense check all candidates likely to be joining the team, they share one key trait – they don't have any desire to waste time on candidates who aren't, on paper at least, in with a chance of getting the job.

So this is the truth bomb – no matter what the self-help business books or 'never take no for an answer' Twitterati say, there are some jobs you're highly unlikely to get – there'll be too many people going for it who are more qualified, experienced, and fluent in the skills required than you are.

That said, don't for one second take that as a mantra to stay in your lane – half the point of changing jobs is upgrading to the next level, putting yourself outside of your comfort zone and leapfrogging other more credible candidates in the process through sheer bravery, gumption, and determination. But you need to have *some* baseline to work with – if you've never worked before, and you're an entry level candidate, then an entry level job is what you should be looking for.

Experience

'The only way to get experience is to have experience' – so goes the tired (but sadly true) tautology. For graduate jobs, internships and placements remain the best way to dip your toe in the water thus lifting your head above the crowd when it comes to candidate evaluation. Luckily, the days of unpaid placements are (mostly) long gone but remain exceptionally hard to gain access to (unless you have a contact who can play the nepotism card for you).

So then what?

Experience in marketing and advertising doesn't have to be formal, and you can design a very exciting background for yourself without relying on luck or contacts.

Built a website in WordPress on a Godaddy.com domain? You've demonstrated self-starting capabilities and entry level web design.

Written words for that site? Congrats – you can draft copy.

Added links to well scheduled, engaging Twitter, Insta and/ or Facebook pages? That's social covered.

Optimised some keywords on the site? Yep, SEO – tick

Drafted a press release and received at least one piece of coverage literally anywhere? PR

Made one sale or had a click through on an affiliate link? Your site is monetised (and you're an affiliate marketer)

Used Google's AdWords tool to drive even just one click to your site? PPC, you got it! Plus, you'll need to have budget awareness and cost control.

And so on. Between learning the 'how' (YouTube videos are your friend here) and doing the graft, the above exercise will maybe take you three days and cost a fiver. The end result of which is you will have demonstrated a real-world capability in seven marketing channels plus you'll be an entrepreneur with the gumption to get off your arse and craft your own pool of relevant experience.

And voila – you've just put yourself ahead of 70% + of other graduate applicants.

Enthusiasm

Some people are naturally exuberant and sail through interviews with a beaming smile and casual joie de vivre.

Lucky bastards.

For most people, an interview is about as appealing as a fungal infection. Your perception and demeanour can shift from calm self-confidence to jabbering wreck, flashes of what's at stake fog your judgement and your ability to recall even the simplest answer gets caught in your throat like a damp sock.

Don't fret – please. Everyone (and I mean everyone) gets nervous in interviews, but take a few minutes to go for a stroll, remind yourself of what they're looking for in the job description and then lock and load your secret weapons – a smile and buckets of pent up enthusiasm.

You really want this job. You've researched the businesses thoroughly. You may not tick every box but you've sure as damnit got the plums to learn fast. You can – and you will – nail it.

And if you get stuck? Wonderful! It gives you the perfect opportunity to pull out your secret weapon – a magazine loaded with laser targeted questions!

Interviewers love inquisitive minds. On the job, they don't want someone who fakes it to make it – they want an active learner – someone who's not shy to expose themselves as a sponge for knowledge. Pull out great questions in your interviews and they can hold more weight than even the most crafted answer.

Emotional Intelligence

'Emotional Intelligence' (EI), 'emotional quotient' (EQ) and 'emotional intelligence quotient' (EIQ) are all descriptors of your capacity to understand your emotional footprint. It's about your capability to recognize your own emotions and those of others, gauging different feelings and managing them accordingly. Ultimately, it's how you use emotive thought to guide your behaviour and interactions with others, and it's a hugely valuable trait.

Some people have a higher natural EI than others, but you can train yourself to be more attuned. Get angry in stressful situations? Temper, recognise and manage that anger, finding optimum outcomes in a calm and rational way. Hi EI people make terrific decision makers and they're also highly intuitive. However impressive their emotional strengths, they're also highly adept at looking in the mirror and being self-critical, meaning they can handle negative feedback, using it as a learning device rather than a personal diss.

The ability to think about the needs of others and responding to their emotional needs are incredibly desirable in fast paced marketing departments and agencies, and as such worth investing time in honing.

How to prepare for an interview

Preparation goes way beyond reading the job description and writing a cover letter. Remember, this is about getting through the door and beating a swathe of competitor candidates, so HR teams are on the lookout for any excuse to exclude candidates at any stage.

Typos are your enemy.

Proof your CV and cover letter three times - then twice more the next morning. One typo is enough to discount you. Seriously.

Test the product – whatever you'll be marketing, give it a go. Easier with an online business than, say, a yacht brokerage but either way, going through the customer journey and taking notes on the good, the bad and the ugly will not only give you excellent interview conversation fodder, but it'll also show you care enough to give a shit.

Talk to people – Linked In or email are the easiest way to reach out to current (or, even better former) employees of the company in question. Ex-staff tend to have looser tongues and are more likely to spill the goodies about what, whys and wherefores of working on the inside. Again, you can hoover up valuable fodder that'll give you stand out in the latter interview stages.

Value you'll deliver to the business

All the above and below elements will help give you a leg up through interview but ultimately the business in question will be looking for individuals who will make them more money.

Ability to learn, emotional intelligence, street smarts, a demonstrable ability to graft, how you solve complex problems, interpersonal collaborative and communication skills all come into play. Your actual cost to the business (namely your salary) shouldn't be a concern –

they've budgeted for this role and are prepared to pay for the best candidate in that bracket, so it's down to you to make the decision an easy one.

Secret Sauce

The magic ingredient to breaking into any marketing job in your early career is, sadly, luck. Hundreds of eager/ desperate competitors fighting for a slightly smaller pool of jobs at any given time. You can make your own by following the pointers listed above but otherwise, it's a numbers game. Some interviewers are better than others. Some are overworked and, as a result, lazy in their questioning and apathetic in their desire to unearth hidden gems in the candidate mine.

You're going to have to kiss a few frogs, manage rejection and grow thicker skin – all of which are exceedingly good practice for when you do land that wonderful first job.

A Word on Perseverance & Luck

As with most desirable careers, marketing is hugely competitive. So many people trying to squeeze into a limited number of roles, you'll almost certainly get to a point in your career when you feel like you've been overtaken to the extent that you're moving backwards. This is normal.

Eerily normal.

So, don't worry – even the high fliers don't have perfect career arcs. Those lucky enough to join the Airbnb's, Ubers and Twitters of this world probably had to kiss a few frogs on their way in. In some instances, luck plays a far greater role than skill, experience, grit, and personality ever could – you'd need to be in the right place at the right time with the right face and be head of the line to close the mintiest of mint roles, so inevitably you're not going to win them all.

Taking a long game view, constantly reevaluating and reeducating yourself and honing your craft in line with your contacts will give you the best shot at success when it comes calling. Yes, a career is a series of bets that either pay off or they don't – the trick is to stack the odds as much in your favour as possible and hope lady luck is in your corner when opportunity knocks.

Chapter 3

Marketing Channels

A brief summary of which channel serve what purpose

"A bullet may have your name on it, but a grenade is addressed 'to whom it may concern". Anon

With respect to this unattributable quote, Above the Line (ATL) covers channels that act more like the grenade – paid and unpaid media that you hurl out into the ether, relying on certain customer segments to see the campaigns, find them interesting and respond to them. Below the Line (BTL) acts like the bullet – targeted media through which you can more accurately seek out your target audience with specific, more personalized creative, messaging and call to action. Per eyeball, BTL is more expensive but being so highly targeted, it converts better. ATL allows you to gain a more substantial reach to a wider audience and is therefore essential as you try and get brand fame and trust in the line of sight of the largest number of consumers.

Research, Data, Insight & Analysis

There's a trope in the marketing world that you're either a data person or a 'gut' person. This is horseshit. The two are as co-dependent as Katie Price and the paparazzi. All good decision making has its foundations in data analysis to some degree so if, like me, you naturally sway towards the creative/ gut end of the spectrum, you'll want to find the best talent in the Business Intelligence (B.I.) and Research departments and stick to them like chewing gum on a shoe.

Research comes in many forms so warrants several hundred cerebral books on the subject alone. The same goes for BI, data, and analytics. In short, they're all about learning more on a subject, be it customers, competitors, media performance, creative, offers or simply what the world's population are thinking and doing at any given moment in time.

Suffice to say, before you go galivanting off to write a brief, strategy, or tactical plan, you'll do a far, far more effective job if you're well informed about the subject at hand (thanks to reams of customer and market research). Then, as your campaigns are running, you'll want results to be analysed in as near to real time as possible thus giving you insights that can be plugged into your next, highly optimized version. Post campaign it's time for the evaluation – often glossed over in the rush to move on to bigger and better things but really, truly essential in measuring where you could've done better and what you'll learn for next time.

Sometimes, the data either isn't available, is not fit for purpose or the path you're taking is so new and original, you can't rely on looking backwards to move forwards. There are some people who spend their careers challenging every strategic problem or tactical roadblock with:

"What does the data say?"

...as if no decision could ever be made correctly without the support of numbers, research, and analysis. Data doesn't always have the answers – at which point you'll remember why you trained your gut to show the way.

As media and creative becomes more attributable the ability to have granular visibility of the what's, why's, when's, how's and what ifs? will only be more essential. If you want to remain competitive, polishing your data and analytical credentials as soon as you can (and committing the necessary time to collaborate with the pros in these fields) will pay back tenfold. But don't forget this goes hand in hand with developing your natural instincts.

A Word from the Pros – Matt Kowaleczko, co-founder, BlueMachina

Data has been a very hot topic in recent years. Apart from traditional applications like Dashboards, Reports and Analyses to support marketing strategy, the rise of AI and Machine Learning opens a whole new world of opportunities.

How to use data in Marketing?

Measure

Make sure you create measurable KPIs for all campaigns you execute that can be easily accessed by your analysts. This will help them in generating valuable dashboards, reports, and insights for you. Monitor how your KPIs compare between different channels, campaigns, and segments to identify areas of greatest opportunity.

Learn

Data can help you in your decision-making process immensely. Run controlled experiments (when applicable, apply control groups to your campaigns) and A/B tests to validate your knowledge, and to learn what works and what doesn't. Statistical testing is a powerful tool enabling marketers to make unbiased decisions. Question your convictions and look for evidence in data.

Predict

In customer acquisition, predictive modelling can help in projecting Lifetime Value of new customers at the early stages, this allows for dynamic adjustment of target CPAs and strategizing.

In upsell or cross sell, predictive modelling can help with understanding which products or offers to use in your campaigns.

In retention, data and modelling can help you in identifying and engaging customers who are likely to churn.

Optimize

Evaluate all your campaigns. Use data and analysis to choose which campaigns to keep and which to change. Adjust your marketing budgets accordingly. Advanced tools like Marketing Mix Modelling and Multi Touch Attribution can help you to understand how particular campaigns or channels contribute to the total revenue generated by marketing.

How not to use data?

Don't think about Analytics and Data like a nice-to-have. Put data at the forefront of your marketing strategy. Don't leave your decision making to chance. Spending large marketing budget without being able to measure how efficiently the resources were allocated guarantees failure. Testing different approaches and learning from the outcome of the tests, on the other hand is the approach practiced by leading marketing specialists.

Avoid cherry-picking of results and recommendations. Don't take campaigns that don't work personally. You won't know the success of your campaign until it's analysed. You learn from every campaign regardless of whether they succeed or fail.

Finally, it is imperative that you collaborate with your analytics department. Brief them on your campaigns and ask them for their suggestions. Work as a team. This will make planning, executing and evaluating/analysing campaigns easier and ran more smoothly. Collaboration will contribute to the success of your company and team.

ATL Channels

TV & Radio Advertising

'Les Grandes Fromages' channels of the marketing world (thanks to their cost as much as their effectiveness), we see and hear ads every day and as fame generating devices, very few successful brands have achieved global fame without TV advertising. Tesla is a notable exception, but if a client or boss ever challenges you to follow their strategic marketing model, take the advice of @GroupThink and tell them you'll get started when they deliver a weed smoking, Mars rocket owning, Billionaire CEO with fifty million Twitter followers.

For everyone else, there's television.

To get under the skin of what makes great advertising work, read the likes of Bob Hoffman and Dave Trott, and follow the work of famed creative agencies like BBH, VCCP, Adam&EveDDB, The Gate, 72andSunny and Uncommon.

Print Advertising

Advertising's aging cousin, sadly less prevalent with the demise of print media. Some of the most intuitive and insightful creative of all time came via printed media, but it's notoriously difficult to hold accountable for even the broadest brand KPIs so unless you're a luxury brand with budget to burn it's less likely to be a priority.

Out of Home (OOH)

See those giant billboards by the side of the motorway? And the ads at bus stops? And the video screens in town centres? These are OOH sites and like print advertising, are designed to spread a brand message to a large, indiscriminate swathe of the population. Good for launching a new flavour of crisps, less effective at selling left-handed golf clubs, so if you need to target your campaigns to certain demographics, whether by age, sex, or user preference then this isn't the channel for you.

A Word from the Pros – Jamie Elliott, CEO, The Gate

Good advertising makes your brand come to mind **faster** and more **favourably** than your competitors, increasing the chances that people will choose it and that your sales/ margins will be increased or maintained.

For the biggest effect aim for **fame**, because fame campaigns are four times more efficient than the rest and outperform on all business metrics:-

- Be creatively surprising to gain attention and inspire your audience to share their enthusiasm on and off-line
- Have distinctive elements like a brand character, strong design elements, a sonic mnemonic or signature music that will ensure your ads are remembered as yours and not your competitors
- Answer the question "what's in it for me?" in every ad - what's the key emotional or rational benefit of your product/service that you should feature because it will overcome the biggest barrier to your audience buying or using it
- Balance broad reach ads creating fame for your brand with targeted activity that is relevant and useful and will tip people into a sale
- Get some expert help, don't do it yourself

For the least effect, here are the things to avoid when building an ad campaign:-

- Pack your ads full of messages. Messages are like tennis balls – throw people more than one they're likely to drop them all
- Be boring – people don't watch boring films or read boring articles, why expect them to engage with your animated PowerPoint slide?
- Don't use all of the data you can to understand your audience: what they feel about your brand, what media (social or otherwise) they are engaged with or what their other interests are

- Don't consider how smart media choices can increase the relevance and impact of your ads
- Don't set objectives or put in place the right methods of measurement to establish that you have hit them – also ensuring you can't optimise as you go or take forward any learnings

(Read 'The Long and the Short of it by Les Binet and Peter Field for more on the benefits of brand building and fame)

Public Relations (PR)

While advertising is a direct transaction through which you pay a media owner to display your creative message to their audience, PR is slightly more nuanced. Good PR professionals will take your brand communications messages and craft a newsworthy story of such value that journalists shudder in their haste to publish it. Being unpaid or 'earned' communications, PR is about a fair value exchange – delivering a story that tiptoes the line between brand message and public interest story. Have a flick through any newspaper and after the headlines a significant proportion of the content will have been fed to the journalists by PR agencies (the clue is in the branded mention). To give fewer interesting stories and added 'umph' PRs will often tie in celebrities in a triangle of value:- The brand gets a confirmed mention in a piece people might actually read, the newspaper gets rich content without having to pay for it and the celebrity gets relevance and a bag of money.

On the less frivolous side is crisis PR and corporate communications – and if you ever find yourself in an utter shit storm of bad press, you'll hope to have a credible PR professional in your corner to advise you as you try and mitigate the damage.

A Word from the Pros - Jo Carr, Co-Founder and Chief Client Officer, Hope&Glory PR

Want to be a future PR guru? Then here's how to do PR well:

- Always be the cynic in the room. The one asking the difficult questions. Is this really new? While it's never nice to prick someone's balloon, in PR you need to otherwise you'll end up with a dud story and no coverage.
- Be ready to act as your client's moral compass. They want to do a campaign around female empowerment but don't have any women on their Board. Then tell them to steer clear. Or more importantly do more to empower woman as deeds are more powerful than words
- Stay curious. Always be a step ahead on trends, on issues, on the national conversation
- Think laterally. You'll often need to think beyond the product or service you've been tasked to promote in order to make it interesting. Be prepared to take your thinking to new places
- Know your media. What works, and in what format – across print, broadcast, online and social
- Be tenacious. If at first your story doesn't land. Try, try again.

How to do PR badly

- If you go native and lose the 'punters' perspective' you'll also lose the ability to truly judge whether something is news-worthy

- Never exaggerate, or lie, or bend the truth. You'll get found out. As simple as that.
- Never reach out to a journalist or influencer without first getting familiar with the type of content they write. You will look foolish
- Never assume. Anything. Whether that's prepping for an event or crafting a story. Second guess constantly, and ask Why? A lot.
- Don't be flaky. Do what you say you're going to do – for your client, for a journalist, for an influencer and do it when you said you would. Much about PR is being able to "make shit happen". If you can't meet a deadline or follow up on a request, you'll never cut it.
- Don't believe the hype. Especially as nine times out of ten you're the one who's created it

Sponsorship

Sponsorship is all about building brand credibility through a relationship with a loved entity, frequently a sports team, TV show or professional body. Getting your logo on the front of a football shirt is going to get your name out there to millions of people and may even generate clicks to your website but the key with successful sponsorship is the exploitation – what you do with the partnership beyond logo placement. Expert advice suggests your sponsorship budget should be shared between the deal and making the most of the deal, with as much as 50% being attributed to each. This might be excessive especially if, like Chevrolet with Manchester United, you spooned £70 million per year on the deal. If you're looking at a more realistic sponsorship deal the keys to success lie in finding a good 'fit' between the entity and your brand, and good deal on the commercials and a long tail of further media ops that will allow you to hit other KPIs beyond brand awareness, including social media access, player access, advertising at the stadia, sampling opportunities and access to their fan database.

Organic Social Media

Tweets, Posts, Retweets, Follows. Insta, Snap, Facebook, Twitter, TikTok. If you're not a twelve year old, I'd firmly advocate employing a professional to lead your social media activity (the 'organic' bit means you're creating social content, engagement, and relationships, not paying for it – which is known, fittingly, as 'Paid Social' - see below).

The problem with organic social is that it *seems* so easy. Post stuff, collect likes and followers, sell them stuff and voila! In real life, this approach will fail, as proven by 100% of brands who have stumbled in without reading the room over the past decade.

Good social media is about delivering compelling content that engages and entertains the audience. That's it. The moment you try and force feed sales messages into your social feed, the audience will clock it for what it is (i.e., not remotely interesting) and dislike you (or worse, ignore you) faster than a Kardashian divorce hearing.

Thus, the need for an expert - however not every brand's tone of voice is suited to zany, intriguing, highly sharable snippets of brain fodder. So, you need to find your niche, invest in creating rich, relevant, and entertaining content in bite sized, snackable formats (video is always well received).

Oh, and as a reminder, employing a young graduate with oodles of social skills to run your social channels might look cost effective but at some point, their lack of experience may be revealed in a huge, credibility damaging mistake, for which you'd have to shoulder the blame.

It's inevitable, but sacking the person responsible would be hugely unfair, so before deploying a super cool social playbook, work on the rules of engagement with everyone from the legal department to the CEO, thus mitigating the danger of apocalyptic screw ups. The trick is a balance of fun, entertaining and reciprocal content that sits, if not directly under your brand guidelines, then certainly complementary to them.

That said, no company is ever entirely safe when working in such an immediate channel as social. In 2017, adidas Tweeted the following:

"Congrats! You survived the Boston Marathon".

...three years after a fatal bombing on the home straight of that very same race.

You're never more accountable than with a channel that goes from zero to global in one click.

Twinned with the outbound content most people focus on with social, it acts as a very open barometer of public opinion, too. Plugging customer service into social channels is now pretty much standard, as anyone who's ever complained about poor customer service can attest. Bitch via email and you're in for a long and usually fruitless wait. Gripe via Twitter and things tend to happen, as flagged by a man who has cornered the market in driving positive customer experience to generate revenue, Jeff Bezos:

"If you make customers unhappy in the physical world, they might each tell six friends. If you make customers unhappy on the Internet, they can each tell six thousand friends".

Experiential Marketing

The swanky word for 'events marketing', experiential and customer experience are any activities that require you to set up a live event specifically to bring your audience and your brand closer together. It might be a party, trade show, VIP trip somewhere, point of sale, product sampling or just a dinner – the point of experiential is that in some guise the guests leave with a stronger emotional affinity for the brand than they had when they arrived.

A Word from the Pros – Nicole Goodwin – Marketing Director (Big Drop Brew Company, formerly at Jägermeister)

How to do experiential marketing well

Make sure there is an authentic fit between your brand and the event

Make sure your target consumers are going to the event

Set smart KPIs for evaluation later

Be sure to have a wish list extra asks – not just about the sponsorship fee – free tickets, tagged social posts, logos on all assets etc

Be sure to negotiate category exclusivity (where possible)

Always do a site visit before agreeing to anything (you don't want to be near the toilets!)

Remember you are creating a memory – give your consumer something to talk about above & beyond the product itself

Maximise your reach by always making sure there is an amplification plan across all your other channels (helps with the ROI)

Make sure your sales team know about the event asap & encourage them to host clients at the event – nothing beats experiencing the brand

Always make sure to carry out a full review and take any learnings to the next event (making it bigger & better!)

How to do events marketing badly

Assume anything …There is a good chance what you assume hasn't been thought about by others

Pay 100% upfront for the sponsorship – both parties have to have skin in the partnership

Use event agency staff – no one knows or lives your brand better than your own staff / agency

Forget to tell everyone internally & externally including your PR agency that you are there

Over complicate the social posts – those that aren't there don't want to see the event they could have been at….more use the budget to spread the word you are there & cement the association leveraging the halo effect on the brand

Evaluate the event purely based on physical people to stand as you won't do events otherwise…it is the Opportunity to see / Reach via the other channels as well

Viral Marketing

Fairly self-descriptive, this one. 'Viral' campaigns are those videos, games, memes or snippets that are so funny/ engaging/ topical/ controversial/ shocking that they're shared by viewers organically (usually by email, mobile messenger or social channels) thus nullifying the need for a media spend. The problems here are twofold.

First, it's impossible to predict whether a campaign will be picked up by masses in advance. It either happens or it doesn't and achieving branded viral success these days is difficult with so much rich content freely available and a general antipathy towards subversive marketing tactics.

Second, the triggers that tend to fuel viral success (funny, engaging, topical etc.) are not freely available in the brand guidelines of many businesses. For example, if HSBC tried to flog a pithy meme if would be briefly chastised by Reddit before being ignominiously shat out. Likewise, should IBM try and culture a TikTok dance craze it would be rightfully scorned with derision. Find the channels that fit, and if you throw enough mud, something might virally stick.

As with any channel, viral media needs to deliver a positive ROI, whether via brand awareness or even better (and significantly more difficult), direct sales.

"Going viral is not an outcome; it's a happening. Sometimes it happens; sometimes it doesn't. Just remember, fans are vanity and sales are sanity." Lori Taylor

Retail Marketing

If you're planning to sell a product in a shop – any shop – then you need to draw on some tried and tested tactics, most of which are founded in the 'Four Ps' of Product, Price, Place and Promotion. Whether you're looking to place a line of clothing in a department store, ready-made chicken dinners in a supermarket, vape juice at the point of sale of a newsagents or hand woven hemp knickers on Etsy, the four Ps will be your tick list of your strategic approach.

As the second part of the process, you need to think extremely hard on behalf of the customer. What do they want, what is their budget, what price are your competitors selling equivalent products for and where in the shop is the optimum location to sell (for example, putting crisps next to the booze aisle is a key trick to attracting impulse snackers as they pick up a six pack).

Finally, the last rule – 'retail is detail'. Thanks to advertising, Google and social media, consumers are incredibly well educated about what's on the market, especially when compared to days of yore, when a cartoon tiger was more than enough to sell breakfast cereal. Understanding customer characteristics, their behaviours, cerebral functions, purchasing habits, payday cycles and the deep seated emotions that influence their buying decision are all critical – it's in this detail that you can go from 'consideration' to the end game - 'sale'.

A Word from the Pros – Guy Wootton, Director of Business at Moy Park

Research to understand how shoppers are interacting with your category:

Having a market structure (decision tree) helps guide what products you place next to each other and understand which are more incremental. Which decisions are pre planned and which are made in store? Placing more substitutable products next to each other in "subcategories" optimises sales and makes the category more logical to shop.

Be clear on what role your category and your product plays for the retailer

If your product is there to drive footfall for the retailer, it will have a very different role than if it is there to drive profitability, or basket size. This in turn will impact your placement in store, on shelf, facings etc... Ensure your view on the role and the retailers' view are aligned.

Make it really easy to navigate

Sounds obvious, but there are more good examples than bad. The faster shoppers make decisions, the more they spend, so make it simple, and use colour/shape to help navigate over words where possible. Use the most well-known 'signpost' brands to assist, even if they're not yours.

And here are some classic mistakes you can make when making merchandising recommendations

Bias

If your recommendations aren't made with the total category sales in mind, you will have zero credibility when making merchandising recommendations. Resist internal pressure to push for your products to be placed onto the eye level shelf or have unnecessary facings.

Trying to interrupt / slow shoppers down

Most shoppers know at least broadly what they want to buy before they arrive at a store and have a goal for how much time they would like to spend there. Helping them navigate to their desired purchase/decision quicker, then gives you permission to offer them trade up or offer incremental options. Of course in some stores, shoppers are there to browse and spend time, but the principle still stands.

Cram too many messages on pack

The brutal reality is that you care an awful lot more about your brand messages than a shopper does, especially when they get to a store. In behavioural economics speak, they are operating in "system 1" where decisions are made in split seconds, so rationalise messaging to the most important.

BTL Channels

Pay Per Click (PPC)

The daddy of accountable media, PPC is used by almost every serious marketing department to some extent (often to a major extent). In simple terms, you analyse your target customer's browsing behaviours, seek out key words and phrases that they're using to seek your product category in their browser then bid to the amount you're prepared to pay for one click on these words via your text ad at the top of their search results page (using 'AdWords' for Google – other search engines are available).

PPC's accountability is also its Achilles Heel – popular keywords (such as 'casino' can cost more than £50 per click (I'm not kidding) and whilst less valuable phrases go for considerably less, good PPC media buying is a cat and mouse game operated at an incredible granular level. You can get an algorithm to do your bidding for you (known as 'programmatic' marketing or 'auto-bidding'), but this remains unproven as a universal solution, mostly due to the high volume of fraudulent or overpriced clicks you can end up saddled with.

Display Advertising & Paid Social

PPC's older sibling, digital display ads are the 'proper' visual media you see on the top, sides, middle, bottom and behind websites (the latter known, jauntily, as 'pop-unders'). You can buy the media space via individual sites or, more commonly, via ad networks.

Paid social ads look like display but within social networks – so any of the sidebar ads in Twitter, Insta, TikTok, Facebook or Linked In.

You need eye catching creative, a great call to action (CTA) and the perfect media plan to find the best websites to park the best ad formats on at the best time. the ability to test, test, test so you can find the sweet spot of all three.

Display is often a wallflower channel – it doesn't get the credit it deserves for driving new traffic. Someone sees a banner, has their interest piqued then searches for more info, ultimately clicking through to your site via PPC or coming direct. This is where attribution modelling comes in – via tags and tracking you can see where the customer has come from on their way to you, then assign (or 'attribute') values to each channel. Display ads may not have been the last thing they clicked on, but they're often the first thing they saw that got them interested, which is invaluable.

A Word from the Pros – Dave Gilbert, Global Gaming Lead, Facebook.com

Advertising on Facebook

While there are several ways to purchase ads on Facebook, most advertisers use the auction buying type - ads are ranked by an algorithm based on their total estimated value for both the advertiser and the target audience, and the 'winning' ad is served to the chosen individual.

Facebook is a complex advertising platform, with many different options that marketers can adopt in order to grow their business.

Below are some basic tips to get you started:

Leverage data sources to improve campaign success

The Facebook pixel allows you to direct your ad at people based on specific actions they have taken on your website. One of the most powerful steps you can take is to implement the Facebook pixel on your site, and then optimize for conversions ("conversion optimization"). This can include anything from visiting a page to completing a purchase. When creating an ad set, you have to choose an optimization event (a pixel event to optimize towards). This choice tells Facebook's delivery system what result to try to get for you.

Choose the right audiences to target

On Facebook, you can use a number of different audience targeting options to find out what works best for your business. These generally fall into 3 categories:

- With the **Core Audience** option, information is pulled from what people share in their profiles and the behaviors they exhibit on our platform. By identifying your Core Audience, you can help more accurately market your campaign to the right people. You can refine this target audience with information such as additional demographics, interests, and behaviours.

- With the **Custom Audience** option, advertisers reach people across devices based on the information they already have access to in a privacy-safe way. You can generate Custom Audiences by using your own sources, such as a customer list, or using Facebook sources, such as Facebook pixel data (website traffic).

- The **Lookalike Audience** option is based on sophisticated modeling which identifies people who share similar likes, interests, or characteristics to your current audience. You can target a Lookalike

Audience if you want to reach new people who are likely to be interested in your business because they're similar to your best existing customers.

While there are a lot of different placements where you can advertise across Facebook, Instagram, Audience Network and Messenger, the easiest option is to choose Automatic Placements: that way, your ad is deliverable through all eligible placements to elicit efficiencies in your ad delivery, helping you get more results for your budget.

Adopt creative best practices

Having creative images with one focal point versus many in product and lifestyle contexts can impact lower funnel attributes such as purchase intent or attributed view content events positively. Similarly, using context type images with one focal point can impact brand awareness positively.

Video prompts both brand and direct response outcomes. Today's video ads are interactive, shorter, and mobile. You can prompt action from videos, when paired with the right targeting, optimization, and call-to-action, which makes it a more functional medium for direct response than it has been in the past.

Based on how people view content on mobile, the following tips for creative design are recommended:

· Create short videos (15 seconds or less) that are designed to capture attention quickly
· Incorporate your brand into the ad early

- Design the ad so it makes sense to people, regardless of whether their sound is turned on or off
- Build for vertical viewing

Static images and video work better together. Direct response campaigns that combine video and static image ads have the highest conversion lift outcomes compared to static-only campaigns. This implies that the two formats may complement each other in messaging and/or attract different audiences.

Optimization of creative can help improve results. Mobile advertisers can use information and insights to fuel marketing strategies. Testing of creative can help you optimize your campaign and can have a significant impact on performance. Optimization can also help to avoid creative fatigue.

Test, learn and reiterate on Paid Social Channels

Facebook reaches more people than any other medium on the planet today and boasts one of the world's most sophisticated advertising platforms. This level of sophistication can be daunting for the uninitiated, but don't be fazed - keep testing new ideas and combinations of data, targeting, creative and placement until you find success.

Search Engine Optimisation (SEO) & App Store Optimisation (ASO)

SEO is how you optimise your site to increase visibility for relevant searches. The higher up the page your site ranks for certain keyword searches, the more likely you'll be to get customers clicking through to learn more about your business above and beyond your competitors.

Search engines (mainly Google) employ bots (imagine them as digital spiders crawling around the web looking for keywords to eat) to explore web pages, harvesting information and storing them in an index. Algorithms then analyse pages in the index to work out the optimum order the pages should appear when a customer is browsing for a particular product or service. It's like a virtual beauty pageant for web pages.

The algorithm is pretty clever and designed with the customer in mind. So if you're looking for a plumber in Cardiff to fix your ornamental fountain, the website of the Welsh plumber who has optimised their site for fountains and has case studies of all their successful fountain work will rank higher than that of their rival who specialises in bidets.

Optimizing the words and images on your site with these factors in mind helps your pages rank higher in the search results. Add to that the benefit of having links from other credible websites (known as PR outreach or link building – see below) and you've scratched the surface of this fascinating channel – get it right and it's the best value acquisition channel out there. It's not a quick fix – it can take months to see the benefit of keyword optimisation or inbound link building campaigns, so you need a degree of patience.

SEO (and its sibling ASO which employs similar tactics to increase rankings in the App store and Google's Play Store) are lovely channels – they're beautiful, really. Creativity, skill, and graft are rewarded with lower acquisition costs when compared to PPC, Display or TV but that's the problem. Everyone else knows that, too – so it's incredibly competitive.

A Word from the Pros – Paddy Moogan, Founder, Aira.net

"In order to do SEO well, you need to keep in mind the core pillars of the channel, which are: -

- Technical
- Content
- Promotion

These are underpinned by SEO not being siloed away on its own away from other marketing channels and product teams, but as closely integrated as possible. This means that when decisions are made in marketing and with product, SEO has a seat at the table, making a key part of your job building relationships with other stakeholders.

Whilst not exhaustive, here are the key points to bear in mind with each pillar: -

Technical

Ensure that your website is crawlable and understood by search engines, whilst providing a great experience for your users, including it being fast and responsive.

Content

Produce the absolute best content that you can for your users, understanding and answering their pain points and connecting them directly to your product.

Promotion

Letting the world know about your content and products by building relationships with key contacts and publications in and around your industry, making them advocates for you and likely to promote you in the future.

To avoid doing SEO badly, you need avoid thinking about it as something that exists independently of other channels. This means that many of the things that you'll do to improve SEO must be closely aligned with what you would do in order to deliver a great website experience and deliver a great product or service - you put your users first.

In the old days of SEO, most websites would win despite not offering the best experience for their users. They would put SEO first at the expense of the user, and it worked.

Now, Google is much, much better at understanding how users engage with a page. This means that the user needs to come first and SEO is a layer that gets factored into this and everything is balanced.

Focusing too much on SEO itself, at the expense of the user, may work in the short term but is a sure fire way to fail long term.

Online PR Outreach & Link Building

If the business face of SEO is on-site, then the party side is online PR and link building - also known as 'outreach'. Google uses many variables in its algorithm to judge what makes a good site and what makes a bad one. Good ones will index higher in any particular keyword search and the onsite stuff (covered above) is what you can do internally to boost your rankings. Additionally, Google cares about what other, credible sites think of you. If they link back to you, that's a good think – so the link building industry was born.

In the early days, this rapidly sank into a pit of depravity – paid links were purchased with alacrity, bags of cash changing hands under conference tables as sites earned credibility the easy but illicit way. Nowadays, Google tut tuts such behaviour, so you need to earn your inbound links by reaching out to credible sites and providing them with appealing content which they pay for with the aforementioned back link. It's a neat and reciprocal process but one which has been turned into an artform of finely honed coverage by specialist online PR agencies and professionals.

Sure, the content may look 'click-baity' but it's bubblegum for the brain that websites gobble up as eagerly as their readers, and the reciprocal benefit of multiple high value links can send a website from zero to hero in a heartbeat.

A Word from the Pros – Carrie Rose, Founder, Rise at Seven

To land high quality links we have to think of it in 3 steps: -

1. What can we do to earn coverage?

2. What can we do to turn that coverage into links?

3. How do we get it in front of right fit publications?

The first step highlights the need for stories and forces you to think like a PR. Stories can be in the form of rich content, data/insight, expert comments, engaging campaigns, or reports. It's something "newsworthy" and relevant that writers, journalists, and editors WANT to talk about. To ensure that ... the data/stories/ content has to be either informative, resourceful, useful, or just completely different.

However, we need links. So how do we turn that coverage into links? By having something on site which adds value to the journalist's story. If they can write the story without linking, completely start again.

And then, selling that content/story to writers at quality sites/news publications in the hope that they cover it and link back. Selling a story is done through press releases, email outreach highlighting why this story would be of interest to readers but can also be done through social media, billboard ads or more. Getting people to see your content/stories is the hardest part, but the other two steps are just as important to ensure it lands and gets links.

How to avoid doing PR Outreach badly

Most people do outreach badly because they get step 1 wrong. The story isn't insightful enough, newsworthy, or relevant and therefore doesn't earn the coverage.

Avoid the obvious, don't be too promotional about your product and think about what your customers are interested in over selling your service and product. Ultimately, we're SEOs, marketers, content creators, creating stories to land links and thinking like a PR is often overlooked.

Customer Relationship Management (CRM)

In very basic terms, CRM is about managing your interactions with customers. In the digital environment your CRM team will pull in user data from everywhere – acquisition channels, the conversion funnel and customer journeys to better define the messages, offers and media with which to communicate with them more effectively.

CRM systems are designed to improve customer interaction and the control of marketing campaigns. They do this by improving efficiencies and interactions across the sales pipeline, often automating communications content, calls to actions and data analysis.

Affiliate Marketing

If you don't fancy doing wide ranging display deals and are keen to be more targeted/ accountable in your digital media efforts, then affiliate marketing may be for you. By working directly with website owners in the sectors you're focusing on you can negotiate tailored rates for every customer they send your way. Typical deals tend to fall in three buckets:

Cost Per Acquisition (CPA) - you pay them a pre-agreed amount for every confirmed (I.e., paying) customer they send you, usually at the end of the month.

Revenue Share - you pay them a % of the revenue generated by the customers they send you – better if you want less risk up front, but you'll lose money on valuable long-term customers.

Hybrid Deals – a blend of CPA and Rev Share – you pay a little bit for each new customer and a smaller revenue share percentage.

A Word from the Pros – Ian Sims, founder of Rightlander.com and former Affiliate Network owner

As an affiliate, I was much more focused on the relationship than the financial reward. Of course, both are important, but I'd rather work with someone I could trust at 20% than someone I didn't know at 40%. My guess is the average was somewhere in the region of 15% after costs and deductions.

Additionally, it wasn't just about the affiliate program. The key to me was that the brand knew how to treat its customers. I was most impressed when an affiliate manager demonstrated their knowledge of the operation's retention tactics and what their product roadmap looked like.

It was also important to find an affiliate manager who understood my philosophy: I liked to spread my risk. I would rotate programs relatively evenly, I never offered 'positions' on my site because I ended up with an imbalance of customers and too much dependency on one program. A lot of affiliate managers couldn't understand why I wouldn't send customers to where I made the most money but ultimately, I wanted to create stability.

Finally, as a rev-share affiliate, I wasn't at all interested in any program that didn't offer lifetime revenue. I was OK with negative rev-share so long as it was clear, had a boundary and the program was solid. That said, if I got in a big hole that looked hard to climb out of, I would either look for a ring-fencing deal or remove traffic until it was clear.

Chapter 4

A Letter To My Younger Self - The Advice I Wish I'd Had

When does middle age officially start these days? Is 60 the new 30? Are Millennials really fast-tracking towards knitting and Ugg boots, bypassing the joyous indiscretions of youth in favour of gluten-free, spinning-class, Guardian-tutting, 'lights out by 9pm' sensibility – all fuelled by probiotic, Bullet-blended, curly kale smoothies and a thousand grains of muesli?

As I creak towards my 40th birthday it's getting increasingly hard to tell what colour-coded stage of life I've reached. I may have no certainty on when I can finally sign out of Skype for good but 17 years into a career in marketing I reckon I've earned the benefit of hindsight and can make a (somewhat) informed assessment as to whether the decisions of my formative years were ultimately for the best. Or whether youthful exuberance and naivety did, in fact, lead me down some avoidable rabbit holes.

If I could email myself as I strutted cockishly towards Golden Square in the summer of '99, here's what I'd have to say.

Don't burn your bridges

We've all been there – a few times at least. The leaving drinks, the final client meeting, the last email before handing back the BlackBerry. You've written a parting shot to all staff and luckily had the presence of mind to employ 'the 12-hour rule' and park it in drafts overnight. But what about now? You're leaving and it would feel so damn good to empty an Uzi of colourful language into their rapidly deflating egos.

But wait. Once the enter button is pressed, how good will you really feel?

Let me save you the risk and ensuing trouble: no good comes of it, ever, in my opinion. I only lit the touchpaper once – an early client, total asshat, not qualified to manipulate Play-Doh let alone multiple drinks brands. I emailed him on my final day in an agency role pointing out his (many and varied) flaws. I spoke of burning bridges and how, if I ever had the misfortune to work with him again my career was already over, and I'd have to become a Hare Krishna instead.

He never replied (probably couldn't work out how to send an email) but that didn't matter. I felt no better – in fact I felt sordid. I'd been paid to do a job, which included managing tough clients, and by sending that one single email I'd fallen at the last fence. I wandered home that night feeling hollow, and very much like I'd let myself down. Take note.

Find an impressive, enthusiastic mentor

Several the most successful people I know across the marketing and gaming worlds, and beyond, have a couple of things in common –

they're extremely bright and incredibly hardworking. They've also often had various doses of good fortune sprinkled over their career along the way. If I were to define an element of how this luck is consistently manifested, it would be the presence of a mentor figure in their early careers.

In most cases it was a boss who guided their development and decision making – and in some cases their first progression to a new firm – whilst embedding solid behaviours that take the rest of us a number of jobs and numerous mistakes to embrace. Find that mentor and follow their lead.

Ask more questions

My big bugbears were contact reports and budgets. Contact reports were skull crushingly boring and apparently pointless tasks that required me to take notes rather than engage with the meetings themselves. As for budgets, well, numbers just left me cold.

As far as Achilles heels go, it's quite a big one if you want to move up the marketing ladder.

However, I was lucky in that I faced up to my initial gremlins, removed my crumbling ego from the equation and asked for help from my then account director. She not only facilitated my practical development but also, in a piece of Schadenfreude yet to be bested, gave me a leaving present I still use to this day – process management skills in the form of ISO9001 auditor training.

The cream rises (and trash gravitates towards its natural home near the bottom)

I wish I could forewarn the younger me about the dreadful people I would come across over a career spanning 13 companies, 10 job titles, six countries and four industries. However, the bright side is that the darkness was ultimately outshone by the light emitting from many terrific, talented, fun, and engaging people.

The truth is dickheads are like coffee stains – every company has them and they're a nightmare to get rid of – but they eventually fade away to nothing.

Don't knee-jerk: if your heart tells you to leave, wait three months before you jump

In your early career especially, the temptation to run back to university and take an eight-year master's degree in kite flying can sometimes feel like a no-brainer. The endless dreary meetings, pitiful salary, late nights working on unwinnable pitches and absurd rent bill to live within an hour of the office simply don't add up. But then you get a glimmer.

The rat race is very much a marathon, so a steady pace with occasional bursts of speed will serve you well.

I remember one low ebb in particular - in my late agency days and inherently unhappy at work I managed to pitch, win, and deliver a tiny viral project for Sony with the help of a couple of creatives and a developer, all working after hours. There was a general fug of negativity around the pitch and on a couple of occasions one of the senior agency figures tried to get me to cease work entirely, on the suggestion that I was soon to be made redundant anyway, but I persevered.

The beer we shared the day of the win was the sweetest validation and an immensely enjoyable (if ultimately hollow) 'screw you' against the agency. I was paid-off and farmed out soon after, but left feeling that at least I'd taken the chance to lead something myself and exit, if not on my own terms, at least with my head held a little higher.

If you can see the bandwagon, you've probably missed it

So. Many. Ideas. One of the most fun things in a marketing career is the opportunity to open the creative gun cabinet and start taking pot shots. I've got a few gigabytes of hard drive storage with everything from dotcom start-up ideas to app concepts, culminating in a fair number of business plans. I even tried to get a few of them off the ground, but if there was one poison arrow that killed more of them than anything else (even more than the stagnating fear of failure) it was that I was replicating – even if subconsciously – ideas, campaigns or businesses that had already been brought to life in another earlier, better-funded guise.

Originality is an elusive maiden but those ideas that stand the inevitable self-doubt and criticism are the ones worth pouring your heart, soul (and most likely savings account) into.

They're as rare as hen's teeth but totally worth the wait.

Managing people well will be your highest priority

When I took on my first account manager role at 25 my father, proud though I'm sure he was at the time, did ask with a certain amount of trepidation whether I'd ever been trained to manage actual people.

In fact, I believe he was more expressive than that.

Back then in agency land, you learned on the hoof – by emulating your boss (if they were decent), collaborating, and trial and error. Mistakes were made – many, many quite cringe-worthy mistakes if memory serves.

Things might have changed – training in management skills may now come as marketing industry standards alongside pointy shoes and a snazzy haircut – but what's certain is your ability to nurture direct reports only gets more important as you progress in seniority. The ever-useful Google is a start point, as are the plethora of books on Amazon. I'd add to that a recommendation to constantly ask questions of managers you respect (remember the mentor); the ones who always seem to get the best from their team and run a tight yet motivated ship.

A product of personal development is that the job you chose as a graduate becomes less about the practical work and more about how you brief, advise, cajole, rein in, and ultimately motivate those who work for you. It pays to take the time required to get it right.

If the offer sounds too good to be true, it probably is

Sometimes opportunity smacks you round the head when you least expect it – a piece of professional good fortune like a bolt of lightning from the depths of LinkedIn. It might be a random start-up offer with a chunk of equity which they swear is worth half a mil already. Or it could be the promotion with a flashy job title that will make colleagues seethe and your friends envious.

Hold fire, champ – time to pause for thought.

Has anything that's been offered to you been guaranteed? Will it be in the contract? Even if so, will the company be around long enough to honour said contract (I can name three examples of firms going belly up around me just as I was due to be paid out).

Sadly, real 'golden ticket' moments are few and far between. What tends to breed ongoing success are the pillars of solid marketing skills twinned with a strong work ethic and a 'get on with everyone' personality. Focus on those and you'll find you'll start to make your own luck.

Measure twice, cut once

It's highly recommended to apply the 'more haste, less speed' axiom to almost anything you meddle in. From PowerPoint to public speaking, take your time and focus on quality over quantity; it's a sure-fire way to appear more professional, competent, and able than your peers.

The grass looks greener – but isn't always

No matter how difficult your working life becomes at times, if you have a job in any area of marketing or professional services it's likely you're considerably better off than the majority. Statistically speaking, you've probably got a university degree, you're able to cover rent (perhaps even a mortgage after a while if you're lucky) and you work among the young and the beautiful in an ever-changing, lively industry.

Be grateful for what you've got and what you've achieved. It doesn't get any easier as you earn greater responsibility, but it does pay better.

Work in what you love – and if you can't afford to do that, do it on the side

There's a utopian dream that we can all achieve nirvana by simply doing what we love for a career. But what if you love painting? Or writing? Or baking? And then you find you lack the talent, determination, confidence, drive, bankroll, or pure luck to make it pay enough of a living wage while you find your feet? If that's the case, then never fear – as that's what evenings and weekends are for.

Time management comes more naturally to some than others but once you have a passion project, it's amazing how easy it is to get up that little bit earlier, to ignore the TV or go out less. You can shave time off pretty much everything else in order to reclaim those lost hours and commit them to something that brings you genuine joy.

It's no surprise or secret than many of those that 'make it' claim that work doesn't feel like work – it's recreational fun that can have the added benefit of payment. Investing time in a beloved hobby outside work is hugely rewarding and a balance to the stresses and strains of your career, so invest in yourself, recapture your passion, and see what amazing things could come of it. It's free to try, and totally in your capacity to have a go.

I wish I'd done it sooner myself.

Chapter 5

Why Should You Choose A Career In Marketing?

Marketing, advertising, PR and all their related and subordinate channels remain hugely desirable vocations and as such, tough to break into

"A lot of times people look at the negative side of what they feel they can't do. I always look on the positive side of what I can do." Chuck Norris

Finishing a university degree is a tense and stressful period in any young person's life. A melting pot of final exams. The pressure of choosing a career path, then finding your first job. And the ultimate prize of having to pay back the exorbitant tuition fees that allowed you to enjoy higher education in the first place.

But in 2020, the year of Covid, things were even tougher, with the uncertainty around whether students would be able to collect a degree at all – and whether anyone would be hiring if they did.

According to TopUniversities.com, some courses were deferred, other students had their degree estimated from coursework and previous exam grades, and some had to sit their finals online. It was a mire, and one that's likely to continue once you switch off daytime TV and attempt to beat the herd to claim your first job.

Meanwhile, agencies and client businesses across the land had to furlough staff, and 'redundancies' was a word being thrown around with the casual abandon of a cliché in a creative brief. These were tricky times, indeed.

But enough of the doom and gloom. Let's park that right here. The world kept spinning and the marketing and advertising industries will survive and thrive, albeit under the banner of their new favourite buzz phrase, the 'new normal'.

So, for the benefit of those graduates who came through from university in whichever roundabout way that eventuated, I'm going to examine whether marketing is still as desirable career as it was when I bullshitted my way to a degree in geography 20 years ago.

Let's have a look at the cons and pros: -

Diversity

In the traditional sense, marketing still has some way to go on diversity, according to the 2020 Marketing Week Career and Salary Survey. The rather woeful diagnosis was that 88% of the 3,883 respondents identified as white with only 4% identifying as mixed race, 5% as Asian and 2% as black. Gender equality data is more encouraging, as 60.9% of all the survey respondents were female, however this is countered by the fact that women are hopelessly underrepresented as you look at more senior positions.

That said, under the second dictionary definition of diversity, that which covers "a range of different things", a marketing career is hard to beat. Unlike other, more staid professions, no two days are ever the same.

It feels like the late, great Terry Pratchett modelled his Discworld universe on the marketing and advertising industries: a large disc resting on the backs of four elephants, standing on the back of an enormous turtle swimming in space.

Cash (part 1)

As a graduate, you may hear the advice from the great and the good in the media that money shouldn't influence your career choices. 'Do what you love', 'follow your dreams' and 'money shouldn't be a decisive factor' are all wonderfully ethereal yet fairly unhelpful nuggets of wisdom – wholeheartedly useless if you have the best part of forty grand in student debt to pay back. This is about compromise – aiming for a job you'll love whilst accepting that a highly paid, desirable position on day one of a marketing career is as rare as rocking-horse shit.

Marketing and advertising salaries start on the low end of professional careers – in part because they're highly sought after, so it's a buyer's market – but progression and associated pay increases are far from linear, so it's worth looking at the long-term view.

So far, perhaps I've not painted the most appealing picture. But hold on – here are the positives.

Creativity

If you have a creative itch that needs scratching but don't have the talent, trust fund or exceptionally good luck to be an artist or writer, then a marketing career remains top of the tree for those whose minds are brimming with fountains of ideas and rainbows of abstract thought. Nowhere else will you have the chance to launch depth charges of brilliance onto TVs, laptops, and phones around the world. It may be brilliance about bog roll, but even those campaigns will make you brim with unbridled joy.

Fun

You're unlikely to engage, interact, socialise, and battle with a more eclectic bunch of misfits in any other career. A smorgasbord of thinkers and doers whose candle burns brightly at both ends.

It's fun – not always, granted – but I can't imagine any other career in which I would have charted a 727 jet on a credit card to go to a beach party in Ibiza, or been in a pop video with Beppe from EastEnders.

Influence

Marketing is about the communication of ideas to influence the thinking and purchasing habits of consumers, so whether you choose to go down the creative, account management or in-house route, you'll have a hand in swaying popular culture – sometimes creating culture from scratch.

It may be for social good via a charity client or something less warm and cosy like 'influencer marketing' or an on-pack promotion. But if you take a moment to consider what external forces affect your decision-making as a consumer on an average day, a great percentage would have started as an acorn of an idea amongst marketing professionals.

Cash (part 2)

Most marketing businesses and departments are meritocracies in which the cream rises. There are agency owners and CMOs who are still in their 20s and, for most people, the chances to progress are directly linked to a blend of brainpower, hard work, collaboration, and a little bit of luck on the way. The earning potential is incremental so if you can stomach the tricky first couple of years then the financial payoff becomes significantly more rewarding.

Internships & Placements

Unpaid placements and internships sadly still exit in some of the less salubrious corners of the creative industries and didn't (as the press will have you believe) peter out with Power Rangers and Pulp.

The 2018 Sutton Trust report 'Pay As You Go?' which looked at internship pay, quality and access in the graduate jobs market stated the sad truth of UK internships quite bluntly:-

- 39% of [UK] graduates in their twenties have done an internship, including almost half (46%) of young graduates under 24.
- Almost half (46%) of [UK] employers report offering internships, with large employers twice as likely to offer them as small businesses.

- Of the [UK] employers who offer internships, almost half report offering unpaid placements (48%). 27% offer expenses only internships and 12% no pay or expenses whatsoever.

Avoid unpaid internships and placements if you can. Please – even if they look like your only option to gain experience in the short term. They are inherently immoral and only used by cheapskate companies exploiting free labour that won't benefit you, your experience, or your prospects in the long run.

There is a plethora of graduate marketing schemes advertised on Google alone. Add in LinkedIn and specialist grad recruitment agencies and you have a start point, but it's still highly competitive.

In this game, the goal is to remove objections to your application as much as it is to shine – getting through the door to impress employers in person should be your sole focus. So take the time to hone your CV, polish your portfolio and check everything three times – accuracy and attention to detail are prerequisites, so typos are punished quickly and mercilessly.

If the traditional grad schemes don't bear fruit then make a list of the 30 or so companies you admire the most and craft a personal, well researched email to the most senior member of staff you can get hold of. Explain your interest in their business and, crucially, where you believe you could add value.

Ask them to meet you for a coffee so you can ask them a couple of questions about their business and how they got where they are, and – voilà! – you've just manufactured a first-round interview.

Futureproofing

Marketing is a necessity. Yes, that sounds like the arrogant assertion of someone trying to sell you something, and it is. Someone will always be trying to sell you something.

Ever since a snake took a stake in apple futures in the Garden of Eden, selling for profit has been a thing. And those with a quiver full of marketing savvy, people skills and commercial nous will not just be able to sell a client's products, you'll be a stone-cold expert at selling yourself, too.

Chapter 6

From Shock To Acceptance, Get Familiar With The 7 Stages Of Job Hunting

Planning a marketing career is not easy, but there's a clear path anyone in search of a new job should follow.

"If you spend too much time thinking about a thing, you'll never get it done." Bruce Lee

Whether agency or in-house, the average marketer will change jobs numerous times in their career – more so than other, more stable industries such as medicine, accountancy, and law.

The median years that salary workers across all industries and trades worked for their employer is 4.6 years, according to a study by the US Bureau of Labour Statistics. However, this longevity varies by age and occupation with the median time spent in any one job for those aged 25 to 34 being 3.2 years. Now, looking at Deloitte's Global Human Capital Trends report, 43% of millennials planned to leave their jobs within two years and only 28% planned to stay beyond five years. The younger generation simply feel there is no 'job for life' anymore and especially in fast-moving creative businesses, the only reliable way to achieve progression or a pay rise is to upgrade jobs between companies.

In such an ever-changing world it's become increasingly difficult to plan the structure and forecast of your long-term career in marketing.

Of course, there is a marked difference between staying within the same company (migrating, relocating or a promotion, for example) and moving to pastures new, however the data above relates to a new job as being within a different business. Marketing folk, it turns out, don't fear change where their careers are concerned.

In terms of the 'ideal' length of tenure, there are many factors at play including age, industry, job level, previous longevity, and market conditions. A 2017 report by the BBC quotes Robert Archer, regional director of HR at Page Group: "In technology, advertising and public relations, where professionals are known to change jobs every few years or even months, job hopping can be considered to be a necessity in order to keep up with changes in the market".

However, before you switch your LinkedIn profile to 'actively looking' it's important to consider what career picture you're painting. In the BBC report, Nigel Heap, managing director at Hays UK & Ireland, warns: "There can sometimes be a stigma associated with job hopping. Constantly moving to new roles without demonstrating a good reason might make new employers wary. They may question your ability to commit to an organisation and it may appear that you cannot adapt to new environments and challenges."

The Deloitte survey is robust, too. It questioned 10,455 young workers from 36 countries born between 1983 and 1994 but didn't look at specific industries. Apocryphally, marketers have short attention spans, and the industry is tight-fisted with its pay cheques in the early years meaning marketing professionals tend to swap jobs more often than a chameleon changes colours at Pride.

Let's consider the career path of 'Sally', a fictional graduate working in a marketing agency in Leeds. Sally is 21 and will retire at the statutory age of 65. Assuming Sally takes 1.5 years away from work on maternity leave and with a marketing job tenure at three years then Sally will have worked for 20 different companies by the time she retires.

This is all ballpark testament, of course. But a cursory glance of my own CV shows six full-time roles and four long-term interim placements over the past 13 years. Add to that four full-time agency positions between 1999 and 2006 and I've managed to clock up 10 'proper' jobs in a 20-year career. Moves were less frequent in the past 10 years with things like shares options and long-term bonuses to consider, but it's still an average of a move every two years.

A study by Luminate Digital looks at the ways in which today's Generations X, Y and Z professionals manage their careers and make themselves visible to potential employers. It suggests that while social tools like LinkedIn remain at the forefront, the cream of the crop have started to shun the constant barrage of spam they receive from recruiters on such networks, instead relying on old school relationships with bona fide executive search professionals (head-hunters to the rest of us) and direct engagement with potential employers.

Having taken paternity leave at the back end of 2018 I decided I wanted to switch back to a full-time role. Running a marketing consultancy from home had its significant merits however I wanted to get back to the coal face rather than advising the geologists on the surface.

Decision made, I pulled the cobwebs off my CV, invested some time polishing my LinkedIn profile and re-engaged with my little black book of recruiters and executive search professionals. Then, I waited for the phone to ring and interview bookings to fill up my calendar.

And then I waited some more.

It turns out that between Christmas, Brexit, and the current market there weren't many C-level marketing jobs out there. Unless you're a B2B SaaS marketer, in which case there are inexplicably thousands. But I'm not (I had to ask what SaaS meant in an interview. For a SaaS product. Interview preparation is so very, excruciatingly important) so I entered what I now know as 'The 7 stages of job hunting'.

Ruthlessly plagiarised from Dr. Kübler-Ross's hauntingly accurate description of human behaviours in the event of loss, my seven stages of job-hunting look something like this: -

1. Shock – "What do you mean you've got nothing? You're [*Insert massive global recruitment firm name here*] - you've got to have *something*?!"

2. Denial – "I've got savings. I'm enjoying being a stay-at-home dad. My golf handicap's improved".

3. Anger – "I had to fly abroad for seven interviews back-to-back. For an interim job. I mean, come on. Seriously."

4. Bargaining – "I don't mind taking a pay cut for the right role. How much? Oooh. Not that much, I guess."

5. Depression – "I've hung my laundry, watered the plants and now I'm writing a stage play".

6. Testing – "I'm certainly open to discussing that part-time position selling the new disruptive hearing aid. In the meantime, I have consultancy briefs to tide me over".

7. Acceptance – "This isn't an easy market – something always comes up eventually. I've just got to be patient and enjoy this period for what it is – time away from the grindstone".

Speaking to executive search professionals to find out why the market is so slow led to responses ranging from the flippant ("It's nearly Easter – always slow this time of year") to the more pragmatic ("You have to feel employers and employees are bedding down, waiting to see what happens with Brexit").

The long-term prospects for marketing careers look slightly rosier. According to a study by the Office of National Statistics, the highly skilled professions of medical practitioners, higher education teaching professionals and senior professionals in education are the jobs most at risk from being made replaced by AI.

In the near term, the professional advice to those of you considering a job change is to keep your powder dry and only move from within the safety of your current job.

Chapter 7

Truth Bombs

Some Brief Suggestions on how not to delude yourself

"You can't build a reputation on what you're going to do." Confucius

If you're hoping to thrive in whichever marketing path you've chosen, there are a few traits, skills or clues that will ultimately mean the difference between a painful struggle and fluid progression. The good news is none of these require heightened intellect – all can be learned or developed.

1. Attention to Detail

The art of formal proofreading has seemingly gone the way of long lunches and dispatch departments (used to manage the sending of artwork to agency clients by courier in days of yore). It remains, however, essential for any marketer, and it is a learnable skill. Having your boss see a typo in a campaign you've produced is bad, but having a client see it when it's live is infinitely worse (trust me on this…). There are some simple steps you can take to mitigate any risk, including:

1. Try to make a break between writing and proofreading – let your brain refresh and look again with new eyes

2. Proofread backwards – this removes the normalcy of reading copy you've read several times and focuses your attention on just the words and grammar

3. Print out the copy and put a ruler under each line as you read it

4. Recognise your usual mistakes – for example if apostrophes confuse you, then do a read through focusing on those only

5. Proofread earlier in the time of day when you're less likely to be knackered/ in a hurry

6. Read everything out loud – it'll slow you down and flag up tiny errors you may have missed

2. Thick Skin

Put money, creativity, and lots of busy people in a pressure cooker environment and sometimes the pleasant aura of calm is going to slip. It might be your unlucky day and you catch the brunt of someone's ire. Or you may have fucked up and a senior figure is angrily ripping you a new one. Whether justified or not you need to be able to let it wash over you and come back for more. Sure, have a quick cry in the bathrooms – totally worked for me when I was given the hairdryer treatment (fairly, in that instance – although the public humiliation was uncalled for – there's much less of that about, thank goodness).

3. Client Awareness

Wherever you end up, the client is the entity that pays the bills, so rightfully they expect you to be well versed in who does what and how they make money. Beyond these basics, you'd be well advised to research the competitive environment constantly, keep abreast of technological opportunities and dive deep into the regulatory and geographic environments they operate in.

There are loads of free resources, data sets and media updates you can get your hands on for free, so in any spare time, devour those.

In short, read more.

4. Pragmatism

Some people are graced with more inherent common sense than others, however pragmatism is definitely something that can be worked on actively. Mapping out problems, speaking to key influencers, planning a path to a solution, and saving time by seeking out process efficiencies are all hugely beneficial.

For example, take meetings. Some businesses are besotted with long meetings. Their collective Outlook calendars are a graveyard of hour-long status meetings and team sessions, an obituary to time needlessly wasted.

Most meetings needn't take more than half an hour, so default to that where possible – and even more would have their objectives achieved if you simply go and have a chat to the person or people involved, either in person or over Zoom.

5. Humility

Nobody likes a smart arse. Sometimes, an insecurity in how little someone knows can be manifested by them pretending to know everything – and it's not a good look. *Nobody* knows everything and you'll soon find the most effective and impressive people you work with will be those who flag the fact that they have no fucking clue what the answer is remarkably quickly. Grab hold of this perceived 'weakness' and you'll skip several years of pretence from the start (see also '10. Ask More Questions').

6. Organisational Skills

The best marketing leaders out there share a few common traits (some of which are on this list). Add to these strategic skills, excellent interpersonal/ management capabilities, and the ability to communicate and collaborate seamlessly and that would be the core skill set of those who have risen to the top. One trait they all share is how they pull everything together, even as the landscape they're operating in is shifting, and this takes a master's degree in organisation. Skills you hone around time, people, and budget management early in your career come back to pay the mortgage later on when you have to juggle multiple unknowns and puppeteer tens if not hundreds of people, ensure each is briefed clearly, understands their role, and pulls in the same strategic direction.

7. Mentorship

I mentioned it in the opening chapters, and I'll probably mention it again later – a lack of mentorship is one of my biggest regrets from my early career, and I paid dearly for this in both time and money several times through ill-advised decisions and career moves. If you're yet to find your first job, reach out to experts and ask for ten minutes of their time. If you've started work, the rock stars in the business will stand out pretty quickly, and most will be receptive to a request for a coffee and a chat.

Make the time count by coming armed not with 'How did you do X?' questions but with proposals for how you plan to do things that they can sense check. It demonstrates your value, inquisitive mind, and initiative, and even though it wasn't the original motive, they'll leave the meeting with a positive impression and memory of someone who stands out and adds discernible value. Collecting fans in this respect does no harm to your progression credentials whatsoever.

8. Patience

Nothing happens overnight. Even the most exceptional marketers, strategists and creatives need time to grow. Sure, some lucky sorts get fast tracked (especially in digital start-ups) but you can't rely on this. Hard yards are the default requirement meaning if, like me, you're in a mad hurry to get ahead of your peers you're going to have to chew on some 'hard to swallow' pills pretty quickly.

9. Bravery

You're going to get rejected. A lot. That's just a given, and if you're an A-Grade student who's sailed through school, university, and sporting success with the gilded sheen of a winner, this is going to sting a little.

Get used to it.

This isn't a game of round pegs for round holes. Every hole has more edges than a jigsaw and there are always shit loads of more qualified people trying desperately to mould themselves to fit in. The bravery you'll need to defeat this early rejection will just be a leather jerkin when compared to the metaphorical suit of armour you'll need later on, when whole campaigns or businesses you've poured your soul into are rejected without so much as a thank you email.

10. Ask More Questions

That's it. Ask anyone, anytime, anything you're unsure of, have an idea about or want to sense check. As an added bonus, clients are tickled by the flattery that comes with being interrogated about their own business. (It's much like dating in that respect).

I asked my peers in marketing what would have been the most influential piece of advice (or thing they would have had access to) when they started their careers. Here are a few of the best:

"1) There's a process for creativity - it's not always "eureka" moments 2) Launching a campaign is nerve wracking and that's totally fine 3) No one wakes up every morning wanting to give your company all of their money, time or attention. You need to earn it". *Fintan Costello*

"What worked today may not work tomorrow. You always have to be thinking outside the box which is super difficult even for people who are 'masters' at it". Dylan Tillman

"If you don't fail occasionally you're not trying hard enough". *Alex Czajkowski*

"If a company keeps shifting agencies, it just might be that their briefs / agency management are part of the issue". *Thomas Rasmussen*

"Try to understand if the statements you're presenting are facts or opinions". *Martin McGarry*

Chapter 8

Getting A Job

"Make sure your worst enemy doesn't live between your two ears."

Laird Hamilton - Waterman, big wave surfer, innovator, and my hero

Crafting Your CV

My first CV was thin, to say the least. Two days' work experience in a Merchant Bank (making coffee and hiding, mostly) and sporadic sessions in a jam factory, putting labels on jars and breaking the lemon curd machine. Nothing to wow any HR department in the land, let alone the world's top 10 ad agencies.

Luckily, content gets easier to create as you add years to your career, but to start with, some hard and fast rules apply. For one, spell correctly. When there are 100+ applicants for any one job, recruiters are itching to find a reason to bin as many CVs as possible, leaving them a long list to ponder, then a short list to peruse in more detail before forwarding the crème de la crème to the department Head.

To make life easier for them (and more labour intensive for you), Applicant Tracking Systems are now commonplace. Effectively these are search engines for CVs – rooting out key words and phrases that match with the job description, thus using raw data to craft an accurate and highly personalised picture of the most highly qualified candida... ha! No, sorry, I can't pretend ATS is anything other than a fool's errand - software designed for lazy recruiters to save them doing the one job they're paid between 10 and 30% of the first years' salary to do.

Not for the first time, employing clever technology to replace human instinct entirely removes all traces of personality, gumption, or natural fit from a candidate's application. It therefore puts an even greater onus on your cover letter to convey exactly why you're the best person for the job, especially when you're applying directly to a brand or agency and bypassing recruiters. Although ATS is annoying, it isn't going anywhere – so as with any immovable hurdle, it has to be overcome.

Which is where the hard labour/ loophole finding comes in to play.

If you have oodles of time available then you can take the job description, pick out the key words from each line of the responsibilities, skills and experience sections and scatter them liberally, like buzzword confetti, over your otherwise naked CV. Then repeat the process for every job you apply for individually.

"But why..." I sense you thinking "...does that help them find the best candidates?"

It doesn't, necessarily. Or it might, but it'll discount a large percentage of potential superstars on the way. Either way, if you want to have a sniff at a first round interview, then you should learn how to play the game. If for no other reason than a number of your competitors will be (plus there are some free ATS tools online that allow you to export keywords and import them into your CV to give you a % match score, which makes this seemingly redundant process at least a little more automated).

I think the increasing use of ATS is simple laziness on the part of recruiters, reducing the efforts and dreams of candidates to ones and zeros, but it's here to stay.

If you don't want to spend hours on every job application you send (and you may have to send many – kiss a lot of frogs etc) then the loophole alternative is to 'game' the system:-

- Copy the responsibilities, skills, and experience paragraphs from the job description
- Paste it on the bottom of your CV, change the font size to '1' and the colour to white
- This tiny invisible pocket of keywords will be picked up by the ATS and score your CV as an absolute humdinger, ensuring you progress to the interview stage where the playing field levels off again

It's a cheat, sure, and recruiters, head-hunters ATS firms will cotton on at some point but finding a job is a numbers game in which you need to do anything in your power to come out as the #1 candidate.

Honing your Cover Letter

Now you've used ATS tools to remove all the meaty bits from your CV, rendering all your efforts to date down to a thin gruel of keywords (don't worry, this isn't the last time you'll be left aghast at the recruitment industry as a whole) you now need to work out how to express them via the medium of your cover letter. But hang on – write a Magnum Opus about how great you are will not only make the reader wince and delete your efforts but also break all rules around humility and self-awareness.

So, a concise, custom-crafted one-page letter is the baseline. Again, hone it to the needs of the business and the role, express humour if appropriate for the job (anything to stand out from the crowd).

Or, to quote Dave Trott (someone who knows a thing or two about such matters): -

"The more fun an ad is, the more likely you are to read it.

The more likely you are to read it, the more likely you are to buy it".

Reiterate any experience that may have been missed in their whistle-stop glance at your CV. Targeting the reader, as with any CRM, is vital – so no 'to whom it may concern' intros. If you can reference the recipient's own work in your letter, and how you might improve it, you're onto a good thing.

You're trying to get a job in the marketing industry, so imagine yourself as the product, your CV and cover letter are the media, and the words are your personal campaigns and Call to Action.

Developing Your 'Personal Brand'

Yes, that phrase is as nauseating to write as I imagine it is to read, but everyone's anonymous until they go above the radar. For creatives, building a portfolio, freelancing, and working on widely shared social projects for the likes of One Minute Briefs on Twitter are all extremely useful starting points.

Building a network of contacts including industry leaders, agencies, brands, and notable individuals is easily accomplished using LinkedIn. Writing posts and articles commenting on the campaigns, brands, and agencies you admire is a great way to introduce yourself and has a handy benefit of acting as background research and juicy discussion fodder for interviews.

Other social media, especially Twitter, will give you an insight into what campaigns brands are launching – plus there's no better way to get under the skin of a digital business than to be a customer – you'll be able to analyse their new user conversion funnel and CRM strategy first hand.

Writing articles, whether on social or industry publications, is very easy. I say easy – if you want to be paid it's incredibly hard but if you have writing skills then most are gasping for relevant content. Pick a campaign or current topic of note, draft your thoughts then submit it to two or three editors in the trade press. You should be able to get a bite pretty quickly and this coverage (in exchange for your efforts) adds another point of difference when you come up for consideration in an interview. No, working for free isn't something you want to be doing (and is luckily vilified in the industry these days) but when there's a fair value exchange it's a different ballgame.

As with many marketing channels, the best way to raise your profile is both targeted and direct. Make a list of the top thirty or so professionals in the field you aspire to work in, drop them a note and ask for twenty minutes of their time. Make a decent impression by demonstrating an intimate knowledge of their business and how you'd go about countering the challenges they face, and not only will you have a new influential fan, but you'll also have bypassed the first stage interview for the next relevant jobs that come up.

Chapter 9

Let's Get Pivotal

Don't worry, you're not going to be stuck in the same job forever...

Covid's subsequent lockdowns were the mother of invention for those looking to shift their careers or start afresh. Picking a route or discipline in marketing doesn't mean you're stuck with it forever – in fact, you're very unlikely to end your career the way in which you started.

Human beings are quite adaptable. We have opposable thumbs, we can communicate in multiple dialects, we worked out complex cognition and we've reached the top of our food chain with room to spare. However, in the biological Champions League of Resilience, we must bow down and worship at the eight knobbly feet of the humble Tardigrade, also known as 'the water bear'.

From the heights of Everest to the Marianas Trench, these cuddly little suckers can be found lurking, getting on with their own (apparently rewarding) lives with the minimum of fuss. At a maximum length of 1.5mm, they aren't going to take over the planet anytime soon but when the sun does explode, these little chaps will be reclining on a deck chair with mini Pina Coladas watching the world burn.

They can enter an almost Zen-like state to deal with environments so extreme they'd make Bear Grylls piss himself. When things get scary, they expel the water in their bodies and reversibly suspend their metabolism, thus entering a state called 'cryptobiosis'. Their only weakness is they can't handle mechanical injury, so you can squeeze them to death.

Pressure gets to all of us, eventually.

It's this level of resilience that we had to evolve throughout the pandemic. It was a bit of a shit time to be a marketer - and not a great time to be working in anything, really.

A huge number of my contacts, friends and former clients were on furlough or made redundant, which was not only sickening for them, but also flooded the job market, sadly bereft of enough opportunities to go around.

LinkedIn, already a last resort for marketing job seekers, became the Wild West with 200 plus applicants for every decent position and as much chance of standing out as an Ewok at a Furry convention.

Global recession is now looking like a 'when' not 'if' eventuality as businesses follow the tried (and frequently disproven) mantra of slashing marketing budgets in order to save pennies – and themselves. For marketers, the aftermath of the pandemic holds about as much anticipatory joy as a dose of crabs.

Luckily, marketing is a career which requires ingenuity, an inquisitive mind and graft – traits ideally suited to navigating the Covid crap cloud.

Adjusting and optimising yourself to your circumstances is known as 'pivoting' and can take one of three forms. In its simplest and most obvious guise, you'll realign your four Ps of Product, Place, Price and Promotion. In my personal circumstances as a marketing consultant who tends to get embedded within businesses for projects or periods, I focussed on PR and crisis management. Bite-sized projects that answer specific client needs and could be packaged small, sold over a Zoom call, and completed quickly so the price would be easy to sign off on. I promoted the repackaged offering to clients and my network and went big on my own PR. The business might not have grown to any great extent, but the leaks were at least plugged to some extent.

For the purposes of transparency, it's worth noting that not all of my pivotal moves panned out so well – namely my Zoom stage play script, esports affiliate website and, most gut wrenchingly, my children's book 'Oink, Moo, Twit Twoo'.

'You miss all the shots you don't take' is a mantra that's meant to make you feel better about such failures.

TL;DR:- it doesn't.

More impressive on the success matrix was the Covid pivot enacted by Greg Anderson, Managing Director of Blue Parrot Events Group. His inspiring story is worth relaying in full:

"For a number of years we've supported the Brightest Star charity and had always sponsored their events. Arlene Smith, who founded the

charity, heard of an appeal by Glasgow Children's Hospital charity for acetate and visors. Knowing we had the ability to produce these, she called us and said it was her time to help us. We're now producing safety screens for offices, restaurants, and beauticians as well as a range of sanitiser units which can be fully branded for a range of industries. This has culminated in the formation of www.sanitiserguys.co.uk".

I asked Greg what the biggest challenges had been when making his dramatic pivot:

"We very quickly had to establish a production line (with extremely limited staff 2 from a 12 initially) and work a way that we could fulfil orders and despatch on time. It sounds easy but when the majority required orders for reopening, there was a huge amount of pressure and a number of late nights to be able to get through orders in time".

Not everyone has the opportunity or capability to make such an impressive and inspiring change at such speed. In another guise, you can simply pivot yourself. Readjust your approach, hone your skills through education, and reposition how you present yourself to the market.

Finally, you can pivot away – taking the negatives of the current circumstances that you can't control and looking for complementary work (or even a charitable/ creative side line) that may not pay as well as what you've become used to but instead ticks many more boxes around your emotional needs – the pleasure centres that tend to be forgotten over a lengthy career in the search for more praise, more money and more power (all things, it's worth noting, that rarely bring happiness).

What you can't afford to do is bury your head in the sand. If the world's best scientists can't forecast what'll happen with Covid next week, then you've no chance. It's more manageable (and waaay better for your sanity) to set small goals, relish the new freedoms we've reacquired and enjoy the process of pivoting in whichever direction and degree that feels most comfortable.

The best thing about marketing as a discipline (and also its Achilles Heel) is that there's never a 'right' answer – opinion is far from binary, and results are the only true measure. This freedom of movement makes *everyone* an expert in a debate with no winners. The same goes for your pivot – there is no right answer so nobody will haul you over the coals for trying something different – especially now.

It doesn't have to be a life changing move - just something to get the blood flowing, keep your brain engaged and add some much-needed excitement to wash away the soup of mundanity we've all have to swim through.

By pivoting into new and untested waters you'll become more resilient, and likely happier, by default.

Chapter 10

How To Write A Marketing Strategy

Trying to teach you how to write a marketing strategy is akin to me telling you what to wear tomorrow and guaranteeing you'll look fabulous.

I don't know your age, size, shape, or sex. With none of that information to hand, my styling strategy has a 95% chance of being totally batshit. Strategy comes last – understanding comes first.

Whether you're an affiliate building and monetising websites from home or a graduate brand manager, on the horizon is the need to create a marketing strategy of some kind.

Traditionally, strategy trickles down from the top. The Board sets out their goals, the CEO works with the C Suite to define how these goals can be met, the department heads will create tactical plans to fit the umbrella strategy, frame KPIs, look at headcount requirements and request the budget they need to make it all happen. The C Suite approves the budget and Kapow! Magic happens.

FYI, this has never, *ever* happened in practice.

In real life, strategic planning for the following year starts in Q3 (the third quarter of the financial year) and bucks like a crack addled bronco until

141

the last possible second when a beaten and bloodied version of the original strategic vision hits the canvas.

The reason it's so hard is because there are so many dependencies, all of which are changing constantly. At some point you have to give birth to your best guess of a marketing strategy, and it's *never* the perfect child. Even if you're a start-up or influencer working for yourself, you'll still need to write out a strategy to show how your brand is going to grow, thrive, make money, and survive.

So where do you start?

Imagine one of those Rube Goldberg machines, used to great effect in Honda's Cog advert and this OK Go video. These chain reaction contraptions are intentionally designed to perform a simple task in an overly complicated way, but in every other respect they represent the crafting of a marketing strategy. Different elements are designed and created before being plugged together to create a fluid entity – the parts connecting seamlessly to deliver forward motion.

Like any good joke, there are a million ways to word a strategy, so there's no failsafe formula. However, most of the ones that end up working will share a process using some or all of these common themes:

1. What's the problem? Have a good, hard, and brutally honest think about what you're trying to accomplish as a business
2. Market Research – find out what your customers are thinking, saying, and doing (include competitor analysis in this bit – don't make life

harder by going heads up against the market leader if you don't have to)

3. Profile and segment your audience – who and where are they and which ones could be most valuable to you? Then go after them first

4. Define your overarching objectives (not too many) and then - only then - start working on your hypothesis and strategy before integrating this across channels within your tactical plan. Channels should support and build on each other (their interrelationships are what make a bog-standard marketing strategy 'integrated') to the extent that the sum should be greater than the parts.

5. Set your targets – 'challenging but achievable' is a pretty good baseline for how difficult/ do-able these should be

6. Always be thinking about what you're planning to do with your 4 Ps: – Product, Price, Place, Promotion

7. Test & Learn - then optimise, changing tack quickly if necessary – 'fail fast' is a great mantra in this respect

Some folks feel the need to craft a Blockbuster marketing strategy. Something that can be summarised in one line (not such a bad thing) and contains inspirational strategic mantras (usually a very bad thing). If you come across a brand or customer acquisition strategy that references 'The Art of War' (originally written by Chinese military strategist Sun Tzu in the 5th century BC) or quotes from films, songs, or Memes, then run. As fast as you can.

A strategy should be concise/ simple, make sense to the oldest and youngest people in the business equally and give you the flex to differentiate from what everyone else in your competitor set is up to. It should also lean on, to a greater or lesser extent, the '4 P's' as originally defined in 1960 by E. J. McCarthy in his book, "Basic Marketing - A Managerial Approach."

Product (or Service) – what is it you're selling? Is it any good? Is there a market for it? How is it branded? Be clear about the features (the things your product does) but focus on the customer benefits (the things your product can do that are needed by customers). It's far easier to market something for which there's an inherent desire rather than trying to polish a turd.

So, to reiterate, product 'features' are all the things your product *can* do, useful or otherwise. A product's 'benefits' are those things that actually answer an implicit need to a particular customer segment. For example, the biggest Swiss Army knife ever made (AKA 'The Giant' - £799.99, fact fans) has one hundred and forty-one functions. But the guy who has a nail stuck in his forehead doesn't need all that. Offer him pliers (with the benefit of nail extraction) for a Tenner, and he'll immediately become a grateful customer buying the right product at the right price.

Place – Where can customers buy your product? Is it well distributed? Which sales channels and locations do your competitors make the majority of their sales in?

Price – This isn't just about being the cheapest. If Moët & Chandon cost the same as a bottle of prosecco, it would lose its unattainable luxury status as well as its position as the world's best-selling champagne overnight. Price isn't always related to cost – it's more about perceived value, positioning and, in the case of luxury goods, exclusivity. Branded corn flakes cost more than a Supermarkets own brand and sell way more volume, despite being exactly the same base product.

Promotion – what's your strategy and supporting tactical plan? What channels will be most cost effective? When is the best time to sell, where are you selling and to which audiences? Do you need to offer a 'deal' to induce trial and subsequent repeat purchase?

That's about it.

In real life, putting a marketing strategy together (encompassing brand, customer acquisition, conversion, and retention elements) is much, much easier if your product works well, has few competitors and, even better, your brand is desirable and differentiated.

It's easy to get distracted by both bullshit and bandwagons when defining a strategy. Trendy buzz-speak and new digital media aren't strategies – they're channels, and often inappropriate ones, no matter how 'on trend' they are:

Influencer Marketing, Shoppable Posts, Immersive, Visual Search, Empathy Marketing, Brand Purpose, Authenticity, On-SERP SEO, User-Generated Content, Internet of Things, Micro Moments, Memes, Voice Search, TikTok, Stories, Word of Mouth, Neuromarketing – the list goes on, and all these things sit somewhere between Tactics, Channels and Content:-

Strategy > Tactics > Channels > Content > Messaging > Call to Action

Take tiny video camera makers GoPro.

Digital cameras had existed since the mid '90s before GoPro got in on the act in 2001, eight years before the first iPhone put a movie studio in the hands of half the planet. Designed to be worn to shoot stills, then video, while surfing or participating in extreme sports, GoPro released the Hero 3 in 2006 with video (but no audio) opening the door to what would become one of the most successful tech strategies in history – delivered, for the most part, through user generated content.

A rich content only strategy is a risk – with fewer paid channels the reliance on self-fulfilling media must have looked scary, but then the purpose of the product – and the output of users – was highly engaging, exciting, and thrilling content, timed neatly to coincide with the dominance of YouTube as an on demand streaming platform. Again it's worth reiterating, this approach isn't for every brand – in fact, only the bare minority will achieve the required reach this way with Touchstorm reporting that only 2% of the top 5,000 YouTube channels belong to brands in 2020.

For GoPro, that wasn't an issue – until it reached critical mass sometime in 2016. Revenues were down 40% and their Karma Drones, the latest in extreme footage capture, started to drop like flies – literally. GoPro did what you have to do in such circumstances – it researched the market, spoke to a wider audience, and pivoted its strategy.

Those potential buyers who enjoyed watching GoPro content and loved the brand had one simple message: "Just show us why we need a GoPro. Explain it to us, make the message simple, and we'll respond. So that was the goal with this ad".

With that, GoPro did what many disruptors had done before it and reverted to TV advertising, showing the one irredeemable trait of all good brands – to jump before you're pushed.

A good marketing strategy is an orchestra. Each channel is an instrument, and if arranged well, they'll play in harmony with you conducting.

Chapter 11

What's The BIG Idea?

A hypothesis is, in short, a likely answer to a problem that you come to after a brief look at the questions. More formally, it's "...a supposition or proposed explanation made on the basis of limited evidence as a starting point for further investigation".

Coming up with a hypothesis is often an early step to uncovering hidden gems of answers to tricky client briefs.

Take this as a case in point:

Early in my career I heard an apocryphal story about an agency pitch that changed my thinking on what marketing and advertising creativity was all about.

The story goes that a gallery in Paris was struggling to attract the city's residents. Tourists were no problem, but with vaults of national treasures and an admissions target to hit, they needed to drive footfall, so they decided to target workers who might want to browse fine art in their lunch break.

The first agency went 'below the line'. They proposed a localised CRM, direct mail, and PR campaign – target individuals who had shown an interest in art, craft stunning creative representing the gallery's storied history, stunning architecture, and priceless artwork.

The second agency went 'above the line' – billboards and radio ads across the whole city and into the suburbs. 'Be proud of your heritage', 'support your local gallery' – that kind of thing.

The third agency went abstract. They sent their agency team to the gallery, had a nosey around, went to the Central Business District and chatted to workers in their lunch break to see why they hadn't been to see all this wonderful artwork whilst munching a sandwich. Their hypothesis was that people weren't visiting the gallery because of geography. It was over the river from the CBD where they worked, meaning it was a twenty-minute walk down the river, over the bridge and back up the other side. This only left twenty minutes of lunch break to browse, relax and nibble their sandwich as they perused the artworks.

With this insight and a fairly clear hypothesis in mind, the agency's pitch was concise – just three words:

'Build a Bridge'

I _so_ wanted this tale to be true, but no amount of digging can find any verifiable origin, but as Mark Twain recognised, "…why let the truth get in the way of a good story?"

Nevertheless, the lessons it teaches are clear:

- Speaking with and understanding the needs of the target audience is a very handy (I understate – *essential*) first step – hearing blockers from the horse's mouth rather than your own assumptions
- Not all answers are obvious
- Abstract thinking is a huge weapon in your creative arsenal
- Not every brief can be answered with a copy & paste channel marketing response (sadly, prescriptive briefing means you'll still just have to do what's asked)
- Giving a client the right answer might do you out of fees in the short term but will often earn your way into their affections (and budgets) in the long run
- Every brief, no matter how inane, needs a big idea in the response. A nugget of insight leads to a crisp hypothesis that's answered by the most comprehensive response.
- Simple is good. Complex is bad. This is always true.

These are creative industries, and your creativity needs to be deployed at every stage of the process – not just the more obvious copy and art direction elements. Crafting an exceptional brief with concise insight, honed research, a cracking hypothesis, and customer centric narrative is the best route to generating great work.

Chapter 12

Starting Out On Your Own

Those who succeed in a marketing career tend to share certain traits. You don't get very far without a decent work ethic, at least a little creativity, some lateral thinking skills, the ability to collaborate with others and thick skin. Coincidentally, these very same traits are common in entrepreneurs, so it's very feasible that at some point in your career you'll at least consider breaking away from the comfort blanket of a salary and start out on your own.

I made the first of my two forays into self-employment in the late 2000s by launching a creative digital agency called 'The Fridge' focussed on the online gambling space. I had an awesome website, retro fridge business cards and what I thought at the time was a memorable strapline ('Keeping Things Cooler for Longer' – eek...). I found a talented designer, developer, and business partner with a track record, found a cheap office in the basement of a dry cleaners, and started hitting the phones.

The industry was booming, there were few (if any) specialist agencies in competition, and I had a decent network through which I hoped to generate leads and subsequently clients on my way to fame and fortune.

TL;DR – it didn't pan out that way.

My mistakes, which were many and varied, might be a useful signposts of what to avoid if you ever answer the call to set out on your own:

1/ Cashflow – ultimately what killed the business, when an (ex-boss) investor changed his mind at the last minute. Without the required client income to keep the ship afloat, I realised I'd have to fund salaries and overheads myself. That was the beginning of the end – The Fridge rapidly started defrosting.

2/ Reading the Room – in my naïve little mind, I was halfway to Charlotte Street – a creative agency founded in the gambling sector, delivering eye catching integrated campaigns and charging top Dollar. Sadly, my clients didn't need that. What the burgeoning gaming world needed was access to fast and dirty PPC, display and affiliate direct response acquisition traffic. Maybe PR and social. I knew that but wanted to persuade them that a brand-led approach would be best in the long term.

Right or wrong, I was stupid to stick to my guns for so long – a rival agency showing me exactly how dumb by flogging millions of pounds of easy, quick, and attributable PPC campaigns to an ever expanding list of operators while I pitched my little heart out to a degrading list of chancers. Confidence is a necessary trait when you work for yourself, but can it surely sting when it's misplaced.

3/ People – when you haven't got the funds to hire the best you need to get creative. I found an exceptional designer pulling pints in the pub under my flat but struggled in other hires. Whether you're starting an agency or building a brand, investing as much time as possible in hiring complementary talent (the best you can afford) pays back many thousands of times over.

There are a few low-cost methods that can be easily employed when it comes to attracting and retaining talent. Thinking about your needs before writing a job description sounds like a foregone conclusion, but people often just dive into replicating a job spec from a previous life without giving due consideration to the *real* requirements. Do you need a costly pro who can start from scratch? Or would a young, enthusiastic upstart allow you to train them into a profitable role? What's the company's brand personality? Is there a natural 'fit'? As much as I abhor HR bullshit, the Insights Discovery (ID) profile tool (initially created by Dr. Taylor Hartman) allows you to measure the people within your organisation by personality type before gauging the types you're missing and back filling accordingly. I've done the ID workshop numerous times and now see it as an essential tool that helps me define how I need to manage different people in different ways. Before then, I thought my 'cover all' approach worked perfectly well. TL;DR – it didn't.

In an ID session, team members (or future hires) are placed in one of four colour coded personality types:

- Red = motivated by power
- Blue = motivated by intimacy
- White = motivated by peace
- Yellow = motivated by fun

Take it down a step further (as you do should you pull your entire team into an all-day workshop of discussion and exercises), and you get a granular picture of everybody's make up.

It's a literal map if what makes people tick - Likes, dislikes, how they manage people, how they like to be managed, what annoys them, what puts them at ease.

It's remarkably effective (if time consuming, and potentially costly) but I'd advocate investing in it as early as possible for the long-term benefit of any new start up.

4/ Flexibility

Nothing ever happens as you plan it. Getting your pants in a knot because your former boss promised to give you some funding before changing his mind isn't going to further your interests whatsoever.

Trust me on this…

Part 2 – The Marketing Bit

In the second half of the book, I've looked at strategy, tactics, and campaigns in the context of the brands themselves, effectively showing how the basics of Part 1 can be deployed (or, equally, shouldn't be deployed) in the real world.

Chapter 13

How To Create A Brand Architecture, Guidelines & Design Style

(…without spending £250k)

I love creating brand architecture books. The name of my old company alone (Brand Architects') is evidence of how much I enjoy honing brands, both old and new. But what I enjoy more than the nuts and bolts of identifying a brand mission, positioning, personality, vision, values, tone of voice and design style is the fact that, if budgets are tight and you're just starting to grow an acorn, the whole process can be done by a team of just one - you.

Creating or refreshing a brand is one of those things that feels like such a big deal it often commands a huge budget and months of planning when in fact this can lead to at best a beige result through compromise and at worst your brand architecture moving in the wrong direction with the wrong content for the wrong reasons.

There's no right or wrong way to go about defining a brand - everything is subjective, albeit there are some best practice methodologies you can employ to define your brand's framework within the parameters of what your customers need and want. Below you'll see some of the methods and process I've found useful over the years to deliver the best guidelines possible no matter what size, market, sector, or evolutionary stage the client found themselves in.

Over the last 18 years I've witnessed the creation of every type of brand guidelines book there is to see. From back of a napkin start-up notes (now a multimillion pound online bingo operator) to a 1.5 million Euro Magnum Opus with a CD Rom embedded in the cover and Astroturf pages ("You must feeeel zee brand, Harry" was the quite frankly outstanding piece of hyperbolic marketing clap trap it was sold with by some mohawked wanker in a hi-art, mid-Euro design agency).

The world's best brands aren't at the top of the recall, respect, and success leader boards by accident. They constantly reinvest in themselves to stay fresh, relevant, and exciting to an ever changing and expanding audience of customers across new devices, markets and through new, ever changing media channels.

Starting with the foundations, a brand architecture book traditionally starts with a Mission Statement. From this paragraph defining the goals and objectives of the brand you expand into a brand positioning statement and thenceforth a brand personality. This triptych acts as a tripod for your brand's tone of voice, copy style and design style to rest upon. Your logo, if it needs updating, is the cherry on top and if you feel a strapline is beneficial in certain media then you can summarise your mission in a catchy manner to appeal to the glancing eyeballs of potential customers.

In simple terms, and depending on your budget, your brand architecture should be built on some version of the following process:

1/ Research Phase - pretty crucial this - understanding a/ where your brand is at, perception wise, b/ what the competitive environment looks like and where the gaps remain for potential exploitation and c/ strategically what direction you believe your customers want you to take the brand. You ask your customers and internal stakeholders a number of questions relating to their perception of your brand

2/ Discovery Phase - I would explore your research and customer journeys, user data, sticking points etc and start to define a series of Workshop agendas. Ideally these Workshops are held with a maximum 15 people in the same room (although I have done a couple with more than 5 offices dialling in by video conference).

3/ Draft Phase - Stage 1 Architecture is defined, specifically brand mission, positioning, personality, and tone of voice. These are then fed into another Workshop session to hone down towards a set of guidelines that are not only accepted by the working group, but largely loved by the majority.

4/ Detail Phase - Logo, font, typography and copy guidelines are defined - either with your in-house design team or an external agency. If needs be, I have a number of design professionals that I know and trust from lengthy experience.

5/ Polishing Phase - Here you debate and chip away at the final draft before putting your new, refreshed brand guidelines into a Brand Architecture Book, or 'Brand Bible' as it's sometimes known. If budget allows then a sense check (via your current customers either through focus groups or simply an online questionnaire) is highly advisable.

The book, on hard or soft form can then be shared amongst all internal and external stakeholders, shareholders, and agencies to better explain what your brand really means, what it's trying to say, how it's saying it and where it's going.

You might be running Apple or (rather more likely) developing a growing business with limited resources. Either way, you have the responsibility to your brand and yourself to create solid, impactful, and relevant brand guidelines.

At the core, your brand architecture is about consistency that conforms that every website, marketing campaign and customer communication looks, feels, sounds, and smells the same. This consistency engenders and efficiency that means people develop a recognition, empathy, and fondness for your brand sooner. This in turn makes your marketing more effective, from initial brand awareness through DR acquisition, conversion, retention and latterly reactivation.

In every media, every day you'll be able to speak with one voice, look the same way and act as a singular entity. And once you're doing that, every single penny of your marketing spend will perform better.

This isn't hard sell sales speak, its universal truth proven by every brand you can name. And all it takes is you and some of the most enthusiastic members of your team spending a few hours in a room with a bunch of customer and competitor research in hand using breakout exercises to bring your ideas to life in the context of your business strategy, target audience and competitive environment.

It definitely shouldn't cost you the £100k + quoted by most brand strategy and design agencies who peddle their wares (and put Astroturf in their brand books...).

So if you think your business is lagging behind and everything you or your marketing team produces feels just a little outdated and disconnected from your customers, then a brand refresh project might be just what you need to inject some life back into the brand.

Chapter 14

Anticipation Is The Way To Keep Customers Coming Back For More

Brands that create anticipation will have a better chance of building equity and the desirable appeal that is sought by consumers.

Dating apps are a lot like champagne. Both categories show how you can build brand value and a compelling user experience by taking advantage of one attribute: anticipation.

A fine bottle of champagne is all about anticipation. It has long been believed by the great champagne houses that more than 50% of their bottle price can be attributed to the value a customer realises before the cork even pops. In the world of champagne, there are good (premium) and great (super-premium) labels. Consistently at the top of the tasting tree is Dom Pérignon, the prestige cuvée of the Moët et Chandon winery.

Purchasing a £120 Dom Pérignon vintage is an event in itself. For the price of 30 pints (20 in the more ludicrous bars of central London) you're making a serious investment, usually for a special occasion.

You're perhaps excited about a forthcoming wedding, birthday, achievement, or romantic sojourn. You want to make a grand gesture, and this is how you might choose to express your love, friendship, pride, or romantic intentions. It also says a lot about your relationship to the recipient – they're not only important to you but they're worth a hell of a lot. They are meaningful.

Presenting the bottle is theatre in its own right. A crowd gathers as the foil is peeled; folks lean in as they await the fireworks of the cork popping. Then, and only then, will you pour out the sparkling magic inside. The inventor of champagne, a rather astute Benedictine monk named Pierre Pérignon, supposedly stated of his new creation: "Come quickly – I'm drinking the stars".

The best visual metaphor ever penned aside, anticipation is key to the champagne experience, and it's the reason the cost of a bottle is so much greater than actual value of the liquid inside. The uplifting, joyful and unquantifiable celebratory experience is a pleasure well before any grape juice passes your lips.

As such, selling champagne's fizzy dream shares many traits with app-based dating. Daters (traditionally singletons, but sometimes not) wait pensively to see what romantic connections might turn up in their futures, above and beyond those they are able to make in the offline world.

Chasing aspirational dreams through online dating starts with a dater's self-perception. The idea that someone is 'out of your league' matters little when you're protected by an app interface, according to a study published in <u>Science Advances</u> earlier this year. Around 25% of those in the online and app dating scene swipe individuals who are perceived as more physically attractive than themselves.

It is anticipation that has driven the incredible growth and incremental popularity of online dating. Every single part of the experience feels like it might be fun.

It's about the 'maybe' of what might happen – and that potential is tantalisingly close to millions of dating app users around the world every day (at the last count, Badoo.com had over 380 million active users globally).

With new daters ready to take the plunge, we can split the options into two broad camps: 'science' and 'volume'.

Science apps, including eHarmony and Match-owned Hinge, determine compatibility based on user data, psychological makeup, needs/wants and preferences.

Apps using the volume model include Badoo, Tinder, Bumble, Happn and Grindr, and present potential dates by interests, age, sex, and location, letting users swipe like a carefree window cleaner until they come across a profile that tickles their fancy.

While Science Apps sound terribly impressive and look terrific on a TV ad to the novice dater, the actual robustness of their model is up for quite considerable debate.

In a 2017 interview with Business Insider, psychologist Eli Finkel (a bona fide expert in the world of online dating from Northwestern University) posited that dating algorithms don't work. The biggest benefit of online dating, he said, is that it puts a shed-load of like-minded people on a conveyor belt in front of you in a simple, user-friendly, and device-compatible format, and hands over the decision-making to the most advanced biomechanical computer known to man: you.

This brings us on to volume dating apps. Take Badoo – as the market leader in this space, Badoo welcomes more than 400,000 new users from 190 countries every single day, who between them send over 350 million messages and add over 10 million photos. In anyone's book the numbers are just extraordinary and, when you put this volume in a UX-enhanced, mobile-enabled, freemium model there's little doubt as to which kind of dating experience the aspirational love hunters of the planet prefer.

The best dating apps today have a user experience to spark the consumer's sense of anticipation and get the heart pumping, and here's how they achieve it:

1. They know the customer, with matches approved by humans, not robots. The ideal dating platform should be able to guarantee that each of its users is genuinely single, so users don't have to worry about their matches having a secret life in another part of the world. It should also verify other details such as age, race, educational level, career, habits (drink, drugs, kinks, etc) and so on.
2. User integrity is key – knowing that a handsome chap isn't a self-obsessed loser with body odour, spaghetti hands and mummy issues

is very, very handy and will save some difficult escape planning. Some apps do this user validation better than others.

3. They present good matches. If it's a tryst you're after, then Grindr or Tinder are likely best suited to your needs. If you're a woman fed up with incessant 'dick pics' from thirsty bros, Bumble levels the playing field. If you want the broadest selection of potential matches who will look like their picture, then Badoo's probably your best shot.

4. Easy does it – this is meant to be fun, not a maths GCSE. A simple user interface with beneficial tools is going to pay dividends in the long term. Nobody wants a billion emojis flooding their inbox, so users look for apps with features that help them filter through the inevitable 'no-men' as quickly and painlessly as possible.

5. Safety first (because, you know, bad people exist). Sadly, there are some nasty folk out there, so the more users know about potential dates before taking the plunge and meet them in person the better.

6. The speed with which you can browse, the chat and video functionality and the choices of available, willing partners make dating apps a veritable supermarket of impulse purchasing. All dating apps are instant introduction tools to some extent, but some have a greater selection within orientations, age ranges and geographies than others.

Online dating seems like a shallow window-shopping exercise with chances of success multiplied by the pure scale of the numbers involved. But romance is an often-forgotten motivation. For all the sexting, Netflix-and-chilling, hooking up and night crawling that dating apps are known and reviled for in the media, the majority of daters are ultimately open to the idea of a meaningful relationship at some point in the future.

Marilyn Monroe, oddly, provides the most insightful quote on this: "Experts on romance say for a happy marriage there has to be more than a passionate love. For a lasting union, they insist, there must be a genuine liking for each other. Which, in my book, is a good definition for friendship?"

Some dating apps will attract more romantic souls and potential life partners than others, but it's the anticipation of romance that – like champagne – gives dating brands their value.

As easy as setting up a dating profile may seem, meeting the love of your life can be anything but. In the same way most of us know the feeling of leaving a teenage party having been universally spurned by the opposite sex, there's absolutely no guarantee you'll meet someone online either. But as Professor Finkel summarised "the most effective way for singles to start a relationship to do is get out there and date – a lot".

And this is where the fun starts – not with the actual first date but with the preamble – worrying over your picture selection, questioning your choice of words in your profile description. What used to be the thrill of the chase is now the joy of search.

For the modern dater, it is anticipation that has driven the incredible growth and incremental popularity of online dating. Every single part of the experience feels like it might be fun. The decision to date online, the profile writing, picture choosing, face swiping, intro messaging, joke swapping, storytelling, date making, out-loud laughing, shy giggling, last orders, first kisses, dreams of what might be.

This anticipation is as magical as it is unquantifiable. It's what some of the world's most valuable brands have managed to bottle. And it's a sentiment never better expressed than by AA Milne in Winnie the Pooh: "Because although eating honey was a very good thing to do, there was a moment just before you began to eat it which was better than when you were, but he didn't know what it was called".

Chapter 15

Did You Do That On Purpose?

Some heavyweight brands tried to flag their woke credentials in response to the #BlackLivesMatter movement - when actions would have spoken louder than words.

Brands that try to attach themselves and their values on to contentious issues such as the Black Lives Matter movement are teetering on a well-trodden and highly perilous path.

It goes without saying that the socio-political situation in the U.S. in 2020 was deeply disturbing. The police killing of George Floyd that ignited the furore was tragic and avoidable, and the Black Lives Matter movement is essential – even if fixing the issue it's been designed to highlight is long, long overdue.

It was back in 2017 in the wake of a white supremacist rally in Charlottesville, Virginia, that black model Munroe Bergdorf took her stand, calling out white privilege, racial violence, and institutional racism. Just a week earlier, she'd been signed as a new face of cosmetics powerhouse L'Oréal Paris – the first transgender model to be offered such a role.

Within days, the brand cauterised its relationship with Bergdorf, claiming that her comments were "at odds with the brand's values of diversity and tolerance towards all people irrespective of their race, background, gender and religion".

This week, following the death of George Floyd under the knee of a white police officer in Minneapolis, L'Oréal shared a post on its Instagram in which it worthily stated: "Speaking out is worth it – L'Oréal Paris stands in solidarity with the black community and against injustice of any kind."

Bergdorf was suitably pissed that her former employer would try to get away with such flagrant hypocrisy and double standards and, as such, she called it out. Her feelings can be neatly summarised in this excerpt from her tweet:

L'Oréal isn't alone. Social media is abuzz with bold, concise, and purpose-laden snippets of worldly wisdom.

Adidas and Nike, two mega-brands with more clout than most media organisations, have collaborated to back the cause and show their disdain for racism, with Adidas retweeting <u>Nike's "For once, don't do it" message</u>. As you'd expect from Nike, the brand that famously found cause with NFL trailblazer Colin Kaepernick in 2018, the digital ad is powerful, moving, and slick in equal measure.

"Woke washing" is not a new nor necessarily ineffective phenomenon, but it appears to have become more prevalent and militarised in the age of social media.

In 2015, Starbucks demonstrated its tone-deaf credentials with aplomb when it <u>asked its baristas to write "race together"</u> on cups to encourage debate about racial oppression following the police shootings of two unarmed black men and the ensuing civil unrest.

Pepsi famously nuked its reputation, almost irrevocably, in 2017 when it tried to piggyback on to Black Lives Matter, implausibly <u>employing model Kendall Jenner to diffuse a race riot</u> with nothing more than a can of Pepsi.

And, last year, Gillette leapt on to the #MeToo movement in a bid to awaken its apparent credentials in the fight against toxic masculinity. It changed its hallowed strapline to <u>"The best men can be"</u> as the suffix to a truly dreadful piece of advertising that men around the world (the lead razor-buying demographic) read, correctly, as a pithy example of nonsensical, headline-grabbing opportunism.

For many brands, the line between showing support for a vital cause and coming across as opportunistic chancers is too thin to feasibly follow without, at some point, falling off. While raising awareness of the anti-racism cause by individuals posting black squares on social media was laudable, the limpet-like efforts of brands to gain kudos in the same way rings hollow – and loudly.

The black square campaign was met with some degree of criticism by activists who felt it was largely performative when posted by people who showed no other support for BLM. There was also concern it shouted over the real meaning of the campaign.

Brands are entities, not beings. Their positioning, personality and tone is decided by committee and acts as the face and voice of organisations, often with thousands of employees and millions of moving parts. They're incapable of sentient thought or human emotion, thus any attempt at conveying real beliefs will ultimately be hollow.

Without a significant historical positioning on the topic in question, brands that raise their benevolent flags in an opportunistic response to circumstance inevitably look like bandwagon jumpers – no matter how slick the execution and moving the copy.

Purpose is something that is earned, not purchased. Hoped for, but not expected. Awarded, not demanded.

Of course, doing nothing in such circumstances feels wrong too. The ensuing blamestorm from the Twittersphere claiming that your brand doesn't "care" enough would drown out any sense in your decision to keep your own counsel.

You can't win – but you can try harder if your brand's historical positioning allows for it.

So which brands are getting it right? Lego committed to donate $4m to "organisations dedicated to supporting black children and educating all children about racial equality". Additionally, it put its money where its mouth is by pulling all marketing materials featuring police figures for the foreseeable future.

In the UK, Britain's own slightly less hip – but no less impressive – version of the Nike/Adidas collaboration came from an unlikely source. Demonstrating succinctly and absolutely that racism isn't everyone's cup of tea, Yorkshire Tea virtually body-slammed a parochial customer on Twitter who had praised its lack of support for Black Lives Matter. Fellow tea-maker PG Tips quickly backed the move with the #SolidariTea Hashtag, tweeting: -

Yes, Jeff Bezos did something similar – but, let's face it, he can afford to lose a few slow-witted customers and Amazon's historical treatment of black, Asian and minority-ethnic employees isn't exactly stellar…

Not every brand has the positioning, history, or balls to take such a forthright and arguably brave stance. However, for those brands that inhabit the middle ground, there are opportunities beyond the generic crud we've seen over recent weeks.

Rather than campaigning your brand's intent and raising its hash-tagged intentions on a digital flagpole, wouldn't a simple pledge to fix what is broken be a more pragmatic and useful solution? Picture this – a plain white post with something along the following lines typed in plain text:

The people behind the world's most powerful brands should ask themselves whether they should have deployed their significant marketing power to latch on to such a powerful cause in the name of brand enhancement, poorly hidden behind the veil of social purpose.

Prompted by recent events and the #BlackLivesMatter movement, we recognise [insert brand name] has fallen short as a business in our duty to treat all people equally. This is something we must rectify.
In recognition of this, we gladly commit the following:-
• 1 week from today, we will share our affirmative action plan
• 1 month from today, we will have started work on every point in the plan
• 1 year from today we will have completed all objectives and will be a better business than we are today
Thank you for your patience while we make things right.

And the answer is no.

Because in context, black lives matter – and brands don't.

Chapter 16

Sometimes, Marketing Isn't The Right Thing To Do

Megabrands like McDonald's and Coke as well as the general public are acting strangely as the world's shifted on its axis. Those that remain more balanced will bounce back faster and in a more positive light.

With the world on quite sensible lockdown due to the Coronavirus, it's hard not to be fearful of future unknowns. Rather sadly, albeit predictably, the fact that we're facing a life-threatening global pandemic hasn't stopped a wave of tone-deaf efforts to jump on the Covid-19 bandwagon, with some brands seeing fit to capitalise on the incapacity, uncertainty and fear sweeping every household.

In 1321, twenty-six years before the Black Death landed, author Dante Alighieri died. Luckily, modern medicine has become less about witchcraft and more about science in the intervening seven hundred years, making it even more dumfounding that people needed a national TV campaign to explain how to properly wash their hands.

Dante wasn't a jolly man (The Divine Comedy is anything but) but even he might want to reimagine the nine circles of hell he described in 'Inferno' in light of some of the codswallop being farted out into the ether, either by brands seeking to polish their godly credentials or by the general public, some of whom seem to have decided a collective lobotomy was an essential medical procedure to demand of an already overstretched NHS.

In Dante's world, the first Circle of Hell is Limbo where the virtuous pagans reside. It's kind of 'Hell Lite' so a fitting home for panic shoppers. As the excellent pop-up website 'How Much Toilet Paper' so eloquently demonstrates, the average hoarder is going to be offloading triple ply until the end of time, and that's without the consideration of *why* bog roll has become the most in-demand grocery item.

The second Circle of Hell is where the lusty make their bed, or in this case, their dinner. For in the great Covid pasta shortage of 2020, it was the sex toy retailer Ann Summers that proved to be an unlikely saviour, selling its famous penis-shaped pasta not for an 'inflated' price, as one might expect, but as part of a threesome for two offer. One can only imagine the uncomfortable silences around dinner tables across Britain as families tucked into their meaty Bolognese…

'Gluttony' is the third Circle. Covid-19's virulent capability to spread to all corners of the globe has only been exceeded by the speed with which celebrities and social 'influencers' have jumped on the bandwagon. From tearful videos shot in glistening neo-Georgian mansions to faux-sentimental sales pitches flogging whatever knickknack is put in front of them, each hash-tagged to the hilt with #StaySafe messages. A whole series of Insta stories were milked, fluffing their #Survivor stories and thanking their Patreon fans for keeping them #Blessed.

In the fourth Circle of Hell are the Greedy. Very few people would consider Sports Direct owner Mike Ashley as modest in either self-esteem nor appetite, and yet his brass balls must be his most flagrant asset. Sports Direct hiked prices on exercise equipment by up to 50% then tried to persuade the government that its stores should remain open. This was roundly dismissed by the Government and Ashley was left to skulk back to his lair to angrily dive, one would hope, into a pool of gold bullion, McDuck-style.

In Dante's fifth Circle, the angry wage eternal battle on the banks of the River Styx. Less far afield, nothing has made me angrier in recent history than seeing the crowds of pissed up tossers outside local pubs on lockdown Friday, enjoying one last hurrah with carefree joie de vivre, casually discarding any concerns about sharing a highly contagious virus with every unfortunate who crosses their paths in the next few months. Tommy Lee Jones summed it up best in Men in Black: - "A person is smart. People are dumb, panicky, dangerous animals".

Heresy, when something is strongly at variance with established beliefs, is the sixth Circle and is in strong supply right now. At the top of the tree was Billionaire PR fountain Sir Dicky Branson, whose Virgin Atlantic airline insisted all employees take an eight-week unpaid leave of absence. Missing the sentiment felt by literally everyone else, Branson's Virgin Group relented last week with a $250 million support package, showing that errors of judgement aren't irreversible, however any genuinely 'good' business wouldn't have to be prompted by public outcry.

'Violence' is the seventh Circle. Fortunately, it seems that mass rioting and looting have been all but avoided as the severity of Coronavirus has been established but there remains a special place in hell for the bottom-feeding assholes who have been mugging NHS staff for their IDs to claim free food for themselves. This crowd will, in a fair world, die a death of a thousand shaving cuts whilst bathing in lemon juice.

In the next Circle, 'Fraud', we can place all companies that decided, in their misguided wisdom, to represent social distancing by putting gaps in their logos. McDonalds even went so far as to *gasp* segregate their famed Golden Arches.

Well, one Golden Arch. In Brazil. For the photo call.

It takes thermonuclear levels of chutzpah to perceive of one's brand so highly that you portray it as Jesus incarnate, saving the world one typographical millimetre of k e r n i n g at a time, but they went ahead all the same, whilst in many cases shafting their workforces.

Dante's final and most hardcore Circle of Hell is Treachery. Many brands deserve to be shoved in here, prioritising self-enriching to the detriment of the very people that keep them afloat in the first place – their employees. McDonald's was a likely candidate but as they already feature, I'll go for Wetherspoons - the 'family friendly' pubco. Led by mercurial Chairman and poor man's Hagrid, Tim Martin, JD Wetherspoon Plc deigned to suspend all pay cheques until they got their government grant at the end of April, leaving thirty-seven thousand low wage staff wondering how to pay for rent and food.

In the aftermath of the Covid-19 crisis the marketing landscape is going to look very different, and the brand autopsy will leave some hollow carcases. Some, as mentioned above, will be reaping what they sow but sadly the majority of businesses that go under will simply be victims of hugely unfortunate circumstances.

While the NHS and its staff deservedly receive the headline applause, a pandemic on this scale needs us all to dig in with real (not fabricated) purpose so we can rise to greater collaborative goodness on the other side.

Brands that try and score points at a time like this will hopefully pay the penalty in customer attrition when the dust settles. The majority of brands will, appropriately, keep their hands clean and try to maintain business as usual, albeit in a highly disrupted fashion.

And those heroic brands that are acting altruistically and without fanfare? You'll never hear about their good deeds because they're likely to be those same unassuming brands you have warm, loyal feelings about even when the world doesn't feel like it's going to hell.

They don't do the right thing not because they have to - just because they want to.

Chapter 17

Don't Hate The Player. Hate The Game

How some Vice industries worked their way back into public favour

"There are things known and there are things unknown, and in between are the doors of perception." Aldous Huxley

As I sat with my daughter at 5am on a morose Covid Monday, time moved ever so slowly.

Switch to the start of the working day. A short commute up the stairs, second coffee in hand and open the calendar. Suddenly it was half one, time to cobble together a toastie before BOOM! Six PM. There was simply no consistency, measure nor reason. Time was slipping by like an eel in a lubricant factory.

It was on a lengthy walk that I came to think about perception, specifically the broader negative sentiments about 'Vice' industries - a hedonistic void I've worked in, on and off, for over twenty years (the last 16 of which have been in online gambling). It's hard to defend gambling as a holistic business. By definition, it involves significant risk and there are certain cohorts of bettors who are at risk of developing problem gambling tendencies.

It's a vice industry with an image problem.

That said, regulated gaming operators aren't exclusively run by evil plutocrats. Most care about their customers and are wholeheartedly behind the majority of pragmatic initiatives that protect players who may be susceptible to gambling addiction. So why is the industry so universally vilified?

To answer that, I looked back to my early career. I spent my formative agency years working for British American Tobacco, Allied Domecq and Budweiser.

Booze and Fags.

Tier 1 Vice industries. The Pros.

Add to these Fast Food, Pharmaceutical Drugs & Petro-Chemicals and you've got the full house of 'naughty' businesses, perceived as the antithesis of contemporary, holistic commercial behaviours.

However, over the last thirty years, the Vice group split. One direction became two. Booze, Drugs and Fast Food peeled away and somehow shed their cloaks of negative perception, leaving the indefensible Big Tobacco, apathetic Petrochemical and perennially slow-to-react gambling industries languishing in the sewers to profit, pollute and wager at leisure.

The Booze industry (led by brand builder in chief Diageo) took control of its own destiny by forming The Portman Group – a voluntary body designed to self-regulate the marketing of Big Alcohol. By taking the reins and neutering government regulators, the industry and associated brands were able to recapture their destiny and today, despite the obvious dangers associated with drinking, they can advertise to adults at will (with health warnings), sponsor sports and cherish a glowing reputation as marketers extraordinaire.

Look at Brewdog. They built a Billion Dollar business by not giving a shit about what anyone thinks of them.

Fast Food took a different path, one driven by product, PR and lobbying as much as brand marketing. Salads joined the menus, dietary information received prominent (although not too prominent) placement on burger wrappers and category leaders McDonalds and Burger King joined sugar chiefs Coca Cola and PepsiCo in aggressive lobbying, both in the USA and Europe.

One such pan-sector effort came in 2004 following the release of Morgan Spurlock's documentary 'Super-Size Me'. A harrowing and amusing film in equal measure, Spurlock spent a month eating nothing but extra-large McDonald's meals breakfast, lunch, and dinner. The burger chain had to respond with a PR charm offensive that eventuated in 'healthier' items being given more prominence on the menu whilst its rivals hid behind the counter to avoid the storm of negative perception. BK went on a mission to reduce the volume of salt in its meals and KFC did eventually introduce its chicken salad. The chicken floggers have since sat on the subs bench for many of the more newsworthy debates around fast food and childhood obesity, but that's not to say they don't have a bucket of ethical batter to dispose of, not least around littering (as I've frequently witnessed first-hand).

Cleaning up their act is something McDonald's have taken beyond the perceptive (lobbying, PR) and product (lower salt content, salads, fruit with kid's meals) and into their customer experience strategy. Famously, one of their key product differentiators in the US was to have bogs cleaned thoroughly and religiously every hour. Older patrons, being in need of a tinkle more frequently than younger, nugget munching customers, would see their pristine khazis on an emergency stop off on road trips, buy some food by means of a 'thank you' and remember both experiences fondly – stopping for repeated visits in the future.

The McDonald's philosophy is proudly displayed on their website:

"Ray Kroc wanted to build a restaurant system that would be famous for providing food of consistently high quality and uniform methods of preparation. He wanted to serve burgers, fries and beverages that tasted just the same in Alaska as they did in Alabama".

To that, they might well have added "consistently pristine shitters" if the juxtaposition of turds and burgers didn't put their gross sales at risk. (It does remain, subtly, in their mantra 'QSCV' – Quality, Service, Cleanliness and Value.

So, time is legitimately great healers, but on its own, it's not powerful enough to create the seismic shifts in public perception required to turn a vice business into a fluffy, acceptable, kiddie friendly brand. In order to achieve Whopper-levels of paradigm shift, you have to change on an atomic level. Product focus, customer centricity and high spending on a relentless public perception mission appear to be the required ammunition. Turn the negatives into positives, grimy products into clean ones, make bad opinions good.

Sure, there are plenty of brands out there faking it with great fiscal success but many of those that are making the most significant strides are also leading their sectors in ethical standards, at least according to 'The World's Most Ethical Companies 2020 report, which put a five year value premium of 13.5% on honourees. Despite some horrific exceptions (such as BooHoo.com) most modern brands derive significant brownie points by nurturing a strong ethical and environmental stance.

The online gambling industry is either going to be sunk beneath a raft of well intentioned (but sometimes misguided) regulation – or it needs to act as one and follow the lead of fast food and big alcohol by bettering itself through improved marketing, customer education/ protection, enhanced product, tactical lobbying, and public perception – and fast.

Behaving well, marketing ethically, protecting customers, doing some good – brand purpose with a commercial engine under the hood. It might sound like some fluffy self-help bullshit, but things have changed. People have changed. Imagine if all of us marketing 'vice' businesses started our strategies with a mantra to 'make things better'. And as a result, public perception would inevitably change for the better.

Then you'd realise that this would almost certainly improve your brand (or your client's brand) performance?

For once, you wouldn't feel sordid about your contribution. You'd feel proud.

Chapter 18

What's Love Got To Do With It?

...and why does Love Island exist?

Love Island is the guiltiest of guilty pleasures for millions of viewers, but why? Money, escapism, and a healthy dose of schadenfreude might have something to do with it.

Love Island (formerly prefixed by the entirely superfluous word 'Celebrity') rears its Medusan head most years on ITV.

It was, as far as I could tell, at 9pm BST on that Monday that the end of days began as a farm of fame rats started flexing their abs and prostrating their vulvas towards a drooling audience of millions.

A few deep breaths and a mellowing dose of Miss Marple later, it occurred to me that I was in the minority. Love Island is a screaming success story of narcissistic guilty pleasure, albeit one that I can barely understand.

In the guise of 'know thy enemy' I realised I needed to gain a better understanding of its popularity. So, I watched an episode.

In fact, no, I didn't – I lasted seven minutes and 52 seconds into episode 44. Dani cried. Jack looked sunburnt (or just ashamed of the lie detector results). Alexandra sobbed. I joined her. Unbelievably, it was worse than I could've ever imagined.

Where had this come from? And why does it exist at all? I felt the need to find out.

We've had due warning, of course. Parody and satire have always been the ammo of choice for the enlightened, and more recently comedians have constantly yet subtly butchered the TV shows that sit in the ethereal mist somewhere between zeitgeist and lobotomy.

Ben Elton took advantage of the fame-diarrhoea factory that was Big Brother in his 2001 novel Dead Famous. That story worked a treat – the format for his other-universe reality porn held the public responsible for killing off contestants if they kept watching. It worked – even in the early Y2K era it rang horribly true but we, the viewing public, reassured ourselves that such absurdity was just a vividly imagined dystopia in our Never future.

Not so now.

It's not the contestants' fault, is it? They're just simpletons who've worked hard on teeth whitening, ethical flushing and sit-ups in order to grab their one and only chance of fame and fortune, battling harsh back stories (like having Danny Dyer as your dad) and a lost cerebral circulation that directs oxygenated blood from their cortex to their cocks.

No, I can't blame them, no matter how unlikable they are – it'd be like blaming mosquitos for malaria.

There's a higher power involved. The puppeteer jangling the strings. Step forward Angela Jain, the managing director at ITV Studios Entertainment.

I'd love to dislike Angela – but I can't. She is, quite simply, a genius. Briefed to produce a low-cost, young demographic, advertiser-friendly televisual Tsar Bomb of filth – she's totally fucking nailed it. Unlike her boss, she won't win a damehood but at this rate she'll be sitting at the same Netflix cash table as Jeremy Clarkson soon enough, which is nirvana for a producer of her capabilities.

Beyond Angela and her ITV bosses (Yes Dame Carolyn McCall, I'm talking to you), we come to the errant advertisers and their media agencies that fund this inglorious drivel.

Superdrug remains lead sponsor – and if anything were to segregate the brand from family-friendly Victorian pharmacy of choice Boots, it's this. It would be great if its involvement related a safe-sex message and enhanced condom sales, but since most contestants think a prophylactic teaches science at university, this is unlikely.

Advertisers clambering to join the bandwagon read as an A to Z of brands trying to recapture their lost youth.

Cadbury's, ASDA, BooHoo, and Ikea feature heavily, with supporting roles for automotive (Nissan and Seat) and technology (Microsoft and Sony) – corporate giants that should know better but just can't help themselves. Kellogg's sponsors the official Love Island: The Morning After podcast and Lucozade sponsors social content ("As shareable as crabs" has yet to go live but it will. It will…)

Meanwhile, a string of product placement deals will see contestants use a heap of branded products on-screen.

Jet2holidays is the travel partner, 90s throwback Ministry of Sound hosts a party in the villa. Samsung is supplying the Galaxy S9+ handsets for contestants to communicate with.

Fashion seems to fit a little better – you can at least flog a floss-shaped bikini or two from Muggy Megan bending to pick up her single brain cell from the pool side, and H&M/ Missguided/ Calvin Klein/ Pretty Little Thing are on hand to sell their wares that way. Primarni will, as ever, flog official, Taipei-produced merch to bejazzled dimwits.

Finally, we reach the bottom of what is a Mariana Trench of a septic tank – cosmetic surgery brands such as MYA and diet supplement Skinny Sprinkles. "Want to look like her? What you need is gastro-intestinal leakage." Yeah, they fit the content pretty well actually. How Dame Carolyn could defend them on BBC Breakfast is beyond me.

Is that it then? The simple appeal of buxom girls being driven back to the Stone Age by guys who struggle to talk and flex at the same time?

No, not quite.

This turgid barrel of medieval pish wouldn't be fathomable without one crucial and seemingly inexhaustible ingredient.

Money.

And here we can understand why a programme so low brow exists. It's hugely popular, socially shareable and drives multi-channel, ever-repeatable advertising fees.

Last year, Love Island's audience was up 73 per cent to two million viewers, and the advertising revenue has become stratospheric as apparently reputable brands claw over themselves to reach the mobile screens of millions of young UK viewers.

Looking at the psychology behind the success, the show's creators have developed a perfect storm of relatable fantasy, escapism, sex, drama and the murky fifth wheel – schadenfreude.

The inclination to enjoy others' failings is a hugely powerful but rarely acknowledged trait (outside media concept brainstorms that is). Rubberneckers gazing on a motorway pile-up are a common example of our innate human instinct to relish the horrific downfall of other people.

Carl Jung stated that our mental health is reliant on our shadow – that part of our psyche that harbours our dankest energies such as melancholia and murderousness. The more we repress the dark, the more it foments neuroses or psychoses. To reach our potential of 'wholeness' we have to acknowledge our most demonic inclinations.

In Love Island the viewer knows the car crash is coming – the format and skill of the editors ensures that. Added to that gleeful anticipation, the perceived beauty and fame of contestants means their inevitable fall from grace is more delicious. Our visual senses are titillated, gossip and backstabbing tickle our need to be 'in the know' and the constant failures of characters to build relationships beyond pool-side trysts feeds our morbid curiosity.

Famed psychologist Eric G Wilson coins it best: "Freud believed that our most basic urges are Eros and Thanatos, sex and ruin. We frequently commingle the two."

So far, so true. But beyond the money and fame, is Love Island just bubble gum for the brain? What of the girls, preening themselves to within an inch of their lives before prostrating their bodies in front of waxed gigolos and banks of cameras? Some may argue they're empowered young women doing what it takes to get ahead in life using their God-given talents (namely large breasts and morals that can dislocate from their selves like an anaconda's jaw).

Before I get too high and mighty, it's worth skipping back a century or so. One hundred and three years to the day before Love Island 2018 hit our collective eyeballs, Emily Wilding Davison, suffragette, and feminist, threw herself in front of King George V's horse at the Epsom Derby. Her actions and sacrifice raised awareness of women's suffrage and ultimately helped win the fight for sexual equality.

What would she make of Love Island? Not a fat lot I wouldn't wager.

With the torturous 'dating prison/ edited torture porn/ advertising click fest' that is Love Island, it seems we're about three years from the metaphysical bottom rung.

Although how we can conceivably get any lower than Love Island is anyone's guess.

Chapter 19

What Marketers Can Learn From Skoda & Japanese Rugby

Japan's rugby team might appear to have few links to Skoda, but both have excelled against expectation using a challenger mindset, which others can emulate.

The Rugby World Cup in Japan was a pristine example of how to stage the perfect sporting spectacle. A fascinating country with a vibrant and ancient culture totally distinguished from the rest of the world, with an enthusiastic population wholeheartedly getting into the spirit of things.

Even in the worrying prelude to and tragic aftermath of typhoon Hagibis, the magical, dynamic, and exuberant joie de vivre of the host nation has shone through, never more so than in the performances of its national rugby squad, who have, almost unbelievably, topped their pool group, beating nominal world number one team Ireland and an improving Scotland on route.

It's worth reiterating that Japan, now ranked seventh in the world, were in the doldrums at 20th as recently as 2006 – this in a sport where any country outside the top 10 is counted as a tier 2 nation, and as such woefully out of contention. Or so we thought.

The Brave Blossoms' hard-but-fair tackling, quickfire offloading and valiant-to-the-point-of-naïve attacking rugby not only won them a place in the quarter finals against South Africa, but also a legion of new and passionate fans – both in the Land of the Rising Sun and in all corners of the world.

As well as new supporters, the upside of Japan's astonishing performances was a renewed confidence to consolidate their faith, skill, and endeavour with which they entered their home tournament. Success breeds success, and so Japan's knockout game against South Africa (a team they beat against huge odds in the 'Miracle of Brighton' in the 2015 World Cup) now looks less like David vs. Goliath and more like a fair go.

This degree of steep ascent from obscurity to greatness is unusual, but not unheard of. It is, however, rare enough to be highly notable when an entity goes from zero to hero in such a short space of time.

Readers of a certain vintage will remember Skoda's 'Phoenix from the flames' repositioning back in 2001. Playing off the hypocrisy of car buyers who recognised the Eastern European car manufacturer's superior value over its counterparts (and then went and bought a Ford Focus anyway), Skoda's strategy was simple. Face its negative perceptions head on, discount them pragmatically through humour and hold a mirror up to the blinkered car buying public who, recognising the cold hard facts, would tacitly admit there was no good reason not to buy a Skoda.

Of any marketing meeting in history, I'd choose to be a fly on the wall at the one in Wolfsburg in the year 2000, when this campaign was sold to Skoda-owner Volkswagen's (VW) top brass by marketing director Chris Hawken and his new creative agency, Fallon. Scenes, one suspects.

Skoda in the early 2000s and this year's Japanese rugby team might not, on the face of things, look like comfortable bedfellows – but they're both courageous, grafting challengers in their own right and share a number of traits that other challenger brands could learn from:

Innovation

In a World Cup dominated by the interpretation (or lack thereof) of the new tackling laws, the 2019 tournament has already passed the record for the most red cards issued in a World Cup. Japan, however, have been notable in their use of more traditional thigh-high and 'chop' tackles, with two or more support players ready and waiting to affect the turnover.

Add to that the startling array of in-tackle offloads they've obviously practiced to perfection, and you have a team that has read the rule book and adjusted their game accordingly.

Skoda's innovations were less of the technical variety and more in brand personality and positioning. Could you imagine a Mercedes, Audi or BMW ad showing a potential customer running away from a dealership in abject horror at the thought of buying one of their cars?

No, they'd sooner add a Union Jack wrap and hanging dice to their rear-view mirrors.

Triumph against adversity

On this point, our two protagonists differ a little. Japan's fantastic team spirit and almost spiritual understanding of each other's capabilities has been nurtured by coach Jamie Joseph and, prior to that, Eddie Jones. The result is a tight-knit team playing for each other and their country with a set of skills that only comes from a total commitment to a shared methodology.

While all but the coldest-hearted have been overjoyed to witness Japan's progress (especially with the typhoon events unfurling around them) nobody was going into bat for Skoda in the late 90s. Their 'us against the world' bunker mentality and a certain 'necessity is the mother of invention' mindset allowed them to create the strategy they did and have the stones to follow through with it.

Nothing to lose

One of the things about being top of your game is that you're afraid to try the unorthodox and take 'hail Mary' risks. If it doesn't work, everyone will publicly pan you, call you arrogant and laugh at your obvious hubris.

Both Skoda and Japan, being underdogs, can look at their options, choose high risk, high reward and ask themselves: 'What's the worst that could happen?'

Diversity

For Skoda, diversity meant a collaborative combination of an eastern European heritage brand owned by Germany's VW with a British marketing director and London based ad agency.

For Japan's rugby team, of the 23 players who recently beat Scotland, only 11 were born to Japanese parents with the balance of the team made up from naturalised Tongans, Samoans, New Zealanders, Australians, and South Africans. Disparate skills brought together under the mantle of one collective team and strategy is, when correctly managed, a thing of irredeemable beauty.

Expect the unexpected

Nobody, and I mean nobody, predicted Skoda's revival from Cold War obscurity to established automotive contender. By the same measure, very few (if any) punters had money on Japan topping their group over established veterans Ireland and Scotland.

The element of surprise is an oft heralded but, sadly, rarely deployed tactic in marketing departments. Yet that's exactly how Skoda and Japan blindsided their opponents.

Sun Tzu worded it better: "Attack him where he is unprepared, appear where you are not expected."

Bravery

Skoda and VW took a giant leap of faith with the 'It's a Skoda. Honest' campaign. They admitted, very openly, that everyone thought their product was rubbish, no more than 10 years after Gerald Ratner had notoriously kyboshed his multimillion-pound jewellery empire when he declared his own products "total crap".

Japan's courage was manifested everywhere in the pool games, from never-say-die tackles to Kotaro Matsushima's two stunning tries against Scotland. This unwillingness to give an inch and total commitment to the collective cause not only made for a stunning exhibition but ultimately ground tier 1 Scotland out of contention.

It's all too easy to accept the status quo. Vanilla marketing strategy, beige campaigns and middle-of-the-road results, leading to a moderate appraisal and adequate bonus, are not to be dismissed. And yet this approach suggests an oversensitive, cautious, and mediocre brand, and a leadership style that's ultimately scared of change. Nothing truly great will ever come of it.

For challenger brands trying to break into the top tier, the answer might lie in less ego and self, more bravery and heart – acting less like special snowflakes and more like Brave Blossoms.

Chapter 20

The Pros & Cons Of Hitching Your Brand To An Influencer

Working with celebrities comes with certain risks, but social media influencers offer an affordable route to fame for canny marketers.

Kids. Animals. To that list you may as well add 'celebrities' as entities you should work with under caution when planning your next big-budget campaign.

Celebs can reap success and insurmountable carnage in equal measure depending on their mood, public perception, behaviour, or which way the zeitgeist is flowing but in today's fame-obsessed world, they're a necessary evil for some brands. Noise-making digital catnip for the masses makes for millions of hard-to-reach eyeballs – these influential narcissists can either be a brand-builders dream or a total nightmare.

It's nigh-on impossible to find an ad that hasn't had its script honed specifically for a star player in the spotlight. In the past you might have been limited by brand fit and budget – the latter of which in turn told you whether you could hire a Hollywood star or a former barmaid from Corrie. Now the celeb barometer goes way past D List and mumbles its way through former pop stars, politicians, and journalists until it skids to an inglorious but timely stop in the gutter of reality TV.

Given the choice, no marketing director would pay the already minted social media celebrity clan a penny more than they already get for simply breathing and talking concurrently, and yet trying to avoid their obvious charms is like saying you'll never drink again after a teenage cider binge. Social <u>influencers</u> are popular – and as such brands need them.

Celebrity does sell. That's the cause and effect of their very existence and there are plenty of great ad campaigns in which the celebrity in question adds insurmountably to the campaign and subsequent brand success.

Think of Helen Mirren for L'Oréal. Her ladyship would only fit the brand better if it cast her body as a perfume bottle. Kevin Bacon, Alec Baldwin and Ryan Reynolds for BT and EE are funny, smart, and self-depreciating – a wonderful coming of age for British Telecom's classic <u>'Beattie' ads of the 1980s</u> with the national treasure who is Maureen Lipman.

Peter Kay 'having it' for John Smiths? Ad perfection – reflected in the beer's popularity during and after the series of ads came to an untimely end.

Looking down the other end of the celebrity spokesmodel telescope there are plenty of high-cost car crashes to reflect on, too. <u>Kendall Jenner's efforts for Pepsi in 2017</u> had all the integrity of a Take That comeback tour. And remember Lance Armstrong? Nike was lucky it had such a deep store of brand equity in its savings account when Armstrong's true colours came to the fore.

The issue remains: if you want to make a mass-market impact, especially as a boring product/start-up/challenger brand then wedding yourself to a star is still the most obvious way – even with the risk it entails.

As with any partnership, selecting a good influencer fit is essential to the success of the campaign and not just for the brand in question. Chris Davis, head of brand partnerships at influencer agency Gleam Futures says: "It's important to understand the brand's objectives and what they are trying to achieve before identifying the right level of talent for them to partner with".

You're also choosing an influencer who reflects your audience - or at least who your audience wants to be.

Davis adds: - "Their audiences are savvy and can easily spot an inauthentic partnership, which will have a negative impact on their opinion of the talent and will damage the strength of the relationship between talent and audience".

Alternatively, you can save your cash (it'll be £20,000-plus, on top of your creative, production and media just to get hold of the tall one from B*Witched – nobody said fame was cheap) and get creative. Use fame to your brand's advantage, for sure, but you can pay Chicken Cottage prices for a Le Gavroche dinner by purchasing fame by association – like bookmakers Paddy Power recently did with the significantly less famous Giggs brother, Rhodri.

To be known as the everyman brother of a millionaire sporting superstar might be considered an unfortunate roll of the genetic dice. To be cuckolded by that same brother must have made Rhodri feel like the unluckiest man alive.

That is, of course, until he was approached by Paddy Power with a sack load of cash and a witty script, and told he had the chance for some very public payback whilst promoting the bookmaker's Rewards Club program.

Rhodri rightfully grabbed the loot, sold out his brother Ryan and has subsequently starred in one of the best below the belt shin-kickings ever seen in advertising. He wasn't a star before (and his price tag would have reflected that) but he sure as hell is now.

The ad is beautifully crafted around the theme of rewards over the overrated and easily broken sentiment of loyalty, with three or four excellent digs about the other erstwhile Giggs brother, who is now known to have played away once more than he should have done.

Maybe this is the way forward? Ignore the costly risk of fallible celebs and go for their grateful, connected and hugely pliable siblings instead. It's a socialist's dream and it might just give us a break from Nicole Scherzinger. We might have run out of Kardashian-Jenners to deify, but they must have a backwater cousin with buck teeth and an unhealthy gator obsession we can wheel out.

Now, the general public is so over-exposed to the unassailable looks of Pop and movie stars that more regular, relatable, and personable types who have also 'made it' via the social channels available to their fans are more desirable and reachable. An image or comment liked or – the holy grail – commented on by Zoella or her ilk is the highest validation; bankable currency that tells the fan that they're not only 'special' but also worthy of the celeb's time.

This closing of the celebrity divide has, as with most things, positive and negative outputs. On the negative side, everyone with a smartphone and an Instagram account thinks that their photos and opinions are worthy of sharing, when of course the vast majority aren't.

On the positive side, social reach can be a force for good. A friend of mine, Seonaid Royall, was trying to Crowdfund support for her RHS 'Believe in Tomorrow' garden – designed to encourage kids to enjoy and engage with nature. I sent a 'Hail Mary' tweet to Nick Knowles, star of DIY SOS, leader of 170,000 followers and all-round good guy, asking him to get behind the project, and within five minutes he delivered.

Nick Knowles ✔ @MrNickKnowles · Mar 11

Looks like a great idea

Harry Lang @MrHarryLang

Good afternoon @MrNickKnowles is this something you could get behind? An RHS garden designed to encourage kids to get outside & engage with nature crowdfunder.co.uk/believe-in-tom... thank you!

💬 2   🔁 3   ♡ 16   ✉

Celebrity is now a collective noun starting with the AAA list (Clooney et al) and ending with the bloke that came second on The Chase yesterday. Everyone has the capacity to have their voice heard on the global platform of social media, and it won't be long before those who refuse to share their every whim online become – like those without tattoos – the exception rather than the norm.

For now, in a world drowning in content, those filled with Botox and an inflated sense of self float to the top.

Chapter 21

Rise Of The Infants

Escapism through esports is one of gaming's great benefits – but it may also lead to societal and addiction problems down the line. The games industry should take this as a warning to protect players.

"All children, except one, grow up."

So wrote J.M. Barrie about Peter Pan in 1911. At the time, it was interpreted as an expression of melancholic fantasy - that children are so innocent that we'd all be better off remaining in a state of blissful naivete rather than thicken our skin with adult fears, regrets, and cynicism. Peter Pan - the perennial arsehole who refused to recognise *any* adult responsibility while flying around letting his friends down - is simply a metaphorical idyll. His lackadaisical meanderings a pipe dream for everyone who fears old age, eschews responsibility, and abhors the progressive march towards their inevitable demise.

We can't revert time – that's the simple truth, albeit one denied by numerous diet programs, cosmetic brands, social media filters, influencers, and plastic surgeons. Beyond the physical wear and tear aging inflicts on our bodies, our minds are under increasing pressure as we stumble through ever more chaotic lives in the digital era - so its perhaps not surprising that technology in the form of esports has become so stratospherically popular so quickly.

These jaw-dropping games and their ethereal digital landscapes offer new, ageless worlds into which you can escape and rejuvenate – pixelated havens within which people can be whatever they want to be.

That is, be whatever they aren't in real life.

For lack of a Holy Grail to extend youth into eternity, esports have come to the rescue - blossoming from niche hobby to global entertainment behemoth in under two decades. Real life is, by definition, boring and monotonous - so 24/7 access to a realm where you can become an empowered, heavily armed hero in the body of an Adonis at minimal expense is, unsurprisingly, desirable to many. Despite the relatively low cost to play, the pure volume of gamers means the business of esports is rich indeed. Research firm Newzoo predicts that by 2021 esports will generate more than $1.6bn in total revenue with $1.3bn coming from brand investments. Additionally, a 2018 paper by Juniper Research forecast that global spending on 'loot crates' and skin betting (that is betting with the weapon wraps, AKA 'skins', within games) would reach $23 billion this year and double to over $50 billion by 2022.

There are now numerous games that could be classed as global blockbusters including Fortnite, League of Legends, Counter Strike: Global Offensive (CS:GO), Defence of the Ancients (Dota), Rocket League, FIFA, and PlayerUnknown's Battlegrounds (PUBG) and a conservative estimate puts the number of esports enthusiasts at over half a billion people globally – and rising. Recent research suggests that in the next few years, esports will have more regular fans than all US sports outside the NFL and globally, esports is well on track to overtake football as the most popular sport to watch within the decade.

Whether esports - a sedentary pastime for both participants and viewers - should be classified as a sport at all is a debate for another forum. What is certain is that whilst there are many positives attributable to the teamwork, coordination, persistence, and skill required to master these games, very little noise is being made about the long-term negative side effects. Days and nights spent in front of two screens, employing three fingers of one hand and two digits of the other, conversing via headset with compatriots and adversaries across the globe whilst guzzling copious amounts of teeth-rotting energy drinks doesn't sound like a recipe for wellness.

In fact, just the opposite.

The potential risks and repercussions were flagged a decade ago by Thomas Weiss in his mouthful of a study 'Fulfilling the Needs of eSports Consumers: A Uses and Gratifications Perspective'.

He examined the gratifications obtained through esports and his studies ultimately highlighted ten need states. Of these, five were competitive (competition, achievement, challenge, reputation, and rewards) which focussed on prosperity through competition and five were hedonic (social relationships, escapism, self-fulfilment, fun and virtual identity) and related to immersion and socialisation.

Looking at these hedonic gratifications, 'Social relationships' is about gaining recognition whilst escapism refers to using the virtual environment to suppress thinking about real world problems and avoid responsibility. 'Self-Fulfilment' describes the satisfaction of individuals' needs for endorsing their own beliefs and attitudes, 'Fun' denotes the perceived enjoyment of players and 'Virtual Identity' mirrors a player's ability to enact different roles and to do things they are not capable of doing in real life.

Of the five hedonic traits, all but 'Fun' should be red flagged as potential dangers, especially in the realm of adolescent and young adult men – a cohort at high risk of succumbing to some pretty unpleasant forms of mental illness including addiction, anxiety, depression, schizophrenia, and bipolar disorder.

'Behavioural addiction' (as an addiction to esports is defined) is increasingly common with an incremental number of cases identified in line with the growth of the esports industry. The brain's reward centres drive a compulsion to play, regardless of any negative impact that doing so may have.

Beyond behavioural addiction, there is significant anecdotal evidence to suggest the catastrophic impact gaming addiction can have on a player's relationships, social life, world view, life prospects and general well-being.

The World Health Organisation estimates that between three and four percent of all gamers are addicted to esports, a number totalling approximately ten million young (under 35 years old, mostly male) players worldwide. If this statistic follows the explosion in the growth of esports even remotely then we're looking at a significant societal problem in the future.

And yet, the problem remains hidden away – it doesn't play well in the narrative for gaming's fervent disciples. Because esports as a business is moving at the speed of light, the pastoral care afforded to young players remains an afterthought – or at least, not as high a priority as bringing esports to the same level in popular hierarchy as traditional sports.

Esports has been one of the few industries to claim a boost from lockdown, with US telecoms giant Verizon reporting a 75% increase in gaming traffic and Streamlabs data showing Twitch, YouTube Gaming and Facebook Gaming usage increased more than 20%. With such popularity comes incremental risk as young men spend even more hours glued to their screens, so it's the responsibility of a number of factions to undertake a total overhaul of how players and fans are cared for and protected: -

The game developers, hardware manufacturers, professional teams and their players, parents, the government, and players themselves must become better appraised to potential dangers, fund research into the negative aspects of the industry and put in place barriers to harm as soon as possible.

Here are a few kick start ideas, taking a lead from the online gambling industry (something I know a little about): -

1/ Warnings about the signs of addictive behaviour at the start of each gaming session, on Twitch streams and links to anonymous resources and helplines for those 'at risk' of gaming addiction

2/ The ability to set maximum session times (e.g. maximum 4 hours in any 24-hour period) when you download a new game and 'take a break' options to allow players to self-exclude from playing for a period of time (with no loss of face/ skins/ kudos). Perhaps even reward players who stick to reasonable session lengths.

3/ Natural breaks in team games with break bumpers offering the opportunity to complete the match later

4/ Player tracking to tell individuals how many hours they've played or watched streams that day/ week

5/ Games that have infrastructure designed with meal breaks embedded in the functionality to encourage shorter sessions and a healthy diet

Beyond the hard effects of potential addiction, the less obvious social implications are harder to quantify but no less relevant. In his excellent book 'Consumed', Benjamin Barber explores the emergence of infantilization amongst consumers, a worrying trend no better represented than in the childlike fantasy worlds of computer gaming: -

"For consumer capitalism to prevail you must make kids consumers or consumers kids … dumb down grown-ups, disempower them as citizens".

Esports aren't a bad thing – far from it. Gaming has been proven to enhance a number of neurological traits including problem solving, memory, multi-tasking and brain speed. However as with anything fun, you can have too much of a good thing. It's ironic that the conservative press gets its knickers in a knot about the amount of blood spilled in shoot 'em up games whilst the actual long-term dangers are more akin to those caused by any other addictive pastime.

Now that esports is a multi-Billion Dollar business, it's overdue to take greater responsibility for the welfare its players and fans beyond lip service. Hopefully the industry can look after its own before heavy-handed legislation and rulemaking become necessary, thus hindering what is meant to be pure, unbridled fun. If it doesn't act soon, more young people will get into an addictive spiral that they'll struggle to escape from.

Unlike Peter Pan, everyone has to grow up eventually - but with regard to young esports players, we need to ensure they reach adulthood in one piece.

For anyone concerned about esports addiction or would like more information and advice on the subject, the NHS has an excellent portal here.

Chapter 22

Creative Awards Remind Brands Of The Need To Take Risks

While advertising awards have little commercial value to clients, they at least remind us that great ads are cheaper and more effective at driving purchase behaviour than relying on outsize media spend.

With the Cannes Lions International Festival of Creativity almost upon us, it's an opportune time to consider the dead certs versus the long shots for a hallowed Grand Prix.

Where advertising, marketing, design, and PR are concerned, there's definitely a chasm between these two camps – and it's one that can be likened to the relationship between nature and nurture.

For anything to be truly nurtured, there's supposedly an actual datapoint to aim for – 10,000 hours. That, if you believe the book Outliers: The story of success by Malcolm Gladwell, is all the practice you need to become a true expert in something.

Fancy beating Serena Williams at Wimbledon? Just don your whites and smash yellow balls for 10,000 hours. Need to master Schumann's Toccata in C? Tickle those ivories for just over 416 days. Have an urge to become the next Stephen Hawking? That'll be 600,000 minutes of your time, good sir.

Perhaps unsurprisingly a 2014 Princeton Study refuted Gladwell's neat but ultimately naïve assertion. Practice, they found, does not necessarily make perfect. Expertise depends on a number of interconnected factors, most notably the base skill and learning capability of the individual. The Princeton boffins suggested that practice alone mattered surprisingly little:

- In music, practice counts for a 21% difference
- In sport an 18% difference
- In education a 4% difference
- In the workplace, a paltry 1% difference

The balance comes from natural talent, the ability to learn cumulatively and determination. But it remains true that you don't get to be brilliant at anything without committing a certain number of requisite hours, no matter how naturally gifted you may be.

In advertising, the nature vs nurture analogy corresponds to the space between creativity and high media spend. Those who lack natural creativity (or the willingness to take risks) might be swayed towards nurturing their brands through big spending in order to reach their goals. Each approach has its merits, and both produce results in their own inimitable way.

The big spend option is the apparent conclusion reached by those brands hellbent on using up a lifetime of hours advertising their wares with adequate creative, in the vain hope that by drowning consumers in sales noise they'll eventually acquiesce through apathy and exhaustion.

Example number one: Peloton. I'm sure you're aware of the 'spinning cycle meets live-streamed personal trainer' business? Of course you are – you can't watch sport on any channel at the moment without being bombarded by its enthusiastic spokesmodel Leanne, peddling its wares with a Haribo family bag's worth of Tangfastic clichés.

"OK, Peloton – let's do this." That's the intro. Then she shows off the personalised UX of the bike's in-built, interactive plasma screen: "David in Edinburgh – that's 200 rides. Let's make it count."

Which worried me somewhat. Can Leanne see all the riders on her screen? Or are you just a name, number, and dollar amount on her bike-mounted spreadsheet? Hopefully it's the latter.

Peloton's massive media spend and glitzy set locations must be why its bikes cost a Lycra-busting £1,995*, paid in monthly instalments – and don't forget you also have to fork out £39.50* per month for the video stream subscription. (*as of in June 2020).

This probably also pays for its celeb endorsements from the likes of Leonardo DiCaprio and Hugh Jackman, once again proving that fads in Hollywood – like cocaine, Kabbalah and, indeed, Peloton – should probably be shunned by anyone east of Pasadena.

Peloton won't be troubling the awards judges at Cannes next week. It has decided on the blunderbuss approach of constantly nurturing a captive audience rather than employing natural creative genius. The brand has been valued at over $4bn, so its chosen path isn't necessarily incorrect.

Also unlikely to be picking up any Lions is the indefatigable Grammarly, which seems to have block-booked every YouTube ad slot from last Christmas to eternity. You can just imagine its CMO walking into Google HQ with $20m dollars in a briefcase. When asked who his target audience was, he simply shouted "bring me everyone!", before sauntering out for a long lunch.

While we're here, the Trivago girl (you know the one) gets a dishonourable mention, too. She gets more airtime than Holly Willoughby and Phillip Schofield combined.

So, there are plenty of non-runners – the bigger, arguably lazier spenders who treat marketing and advertising as siege warfare. There are, however, plenty of ad land's finest currently steam-cleaning their ivory linen suits and buffing the pennies in their loafers, ready to decamp to the south of France, hoping their creative genius will finally receive the long overdue recognition it deserves.

Those agencies on the shortlists tend to follow the path of nature rather than nurture – simplicity in strategic thinking, organic communication, pure copy, natural intelligence leading to intelligent design.

Look at some of last year's <u>winners</u> and you see sheer genius emanating from every pixel. These campaigns are so strong they would have gone viral in the 1860s, shared by excited factory urchins via scraps of newsprint.

For all this creative brilliance, though, is there still a point in these awards beyond individual and agency ego? Having been both sides of the agency/ client fence I know that for an agency there's great PR boon to winning, plus there's the significant career boost that a trophy can offer a creative team.

On the client side, it's harder to commercially justify the effort and cost that goes into winning an award. After the obligatory social post, internal mailshot and press release that everyone ignores, the silverware tends to sit morosely in glass cabinets of reception areas gathering dust – a reminder of a time long forgotten when you were a brave business with great agencies doing challenging work.

That said, we exist in a data-dependent place now in which the nurturing of metrics and analysis often gets the nod over gut-feel, sixth sense and cojones.

Creative awards are an objective reminder that you can still motivate customers by tickling their decision-making parts on a more emotional (and cheaper) level without the need the bludgeon them into a flaccid submission with a barrage of hard-sell noise.

For that reason alone, we should be glad they exist.

Chapter 23

Making The Most Of Conferences

An A to Z Guide

Here are a few pointers to get more out of your time at industry conferences, whether as a speaker, delegate or show pony: -

Advanced planning – the yearly budget review gets most of us thinking about which conferences to go to and which to skip. It's also when you can start negotiating for better multi-show deals, better floor positions and added value stuff like hanging banner branding. Last minute panic shopping is a nightmare, trust me...

Breakfast – the most important meal of the day, it's often said, and never more so when you're going to be on your feet for eight hours in daylight and probably more at night.

Calendar – whether Outlook, Google or a printed Excel sheet try to avoid overbooking yourself with meetings. Some inevitably overrun and half the point of a conference is the ability to wander the floor and have unplanned conversations with potential leads.

Drinking – things have moved on in terms of the work/ play balance but we're still an industry that enjoys burning a candle at both ends. If you're young enough to hit the parties and still be switching the stand on at 9AM then all credit to you, but I'd suggest front-loading your meeting schedule to leave a more mellow schedule towards the end of the show.

Event Manager – They own the show, but despite the fact that you've paid a fortune to have your own slice of real estate you're not the most important person in the room. Be nice to them and when the inevitable calamity happens or your Wi-Fi drops off, they'll be much more likely to go out of their way to do you a solid.

Flight times – unless you work for yourself or the tightest of low budget start up you don't have to get the cheapest flight in. You'll never be at your best if you start a show after 4 hours sleep and a 4AM flight.

Giveaways – USB sticks, free pens, iPads – don't put them in a bowl at the front of your stand – there are numerous punters who probably don't even work in the industry who trawl conferences collecting freebies. Instead I'd suggest having one big stand-out branded prize and doing a draw from all the meetings and contacts you made during the event, ensuring you get their correct contact details.

Hotels Vs. Apartments – I personally favour the value offered by a luxury Airbnb near the conference venue. Less costly and more homely than a hotel with the added benefit you can have a remote office set up so you and your team can work pre and post conference. In Barcelona I once found a converted tugboat with party terrace for half the price of four hotel rooms, so don't be afraid of getting creative with your digs.

Jealousy – More often than not a well-designed 3x3 stand with adequate seating space will fit your needs perfectly and give you change from $15k to set up in its entirety.

Know Your Customer – KYC isn't just for anti-fraud – be sure to strike a balance between generating new business and taking time to meet with your current base. They're being aggressively targeted by your competitors at the very same event, so show them some love.

Lunch – by 1PM you and your team will be getting into sugar crash territory. Make sure you, your team and your promotional staff are fed and watered in good time. It's always a good idea to cover the cost too – it generates valuable good will and they'll be more likely to go the extra mile for you.

Models – we're seeing less near-nude body painted promo models these days, but this outdated trend hasn't, sadly, been buried for good yet. It's 2021, for crying out loud – enough, already. If you want to use promo girls, dress them smartly, brief them well, incentivise them to drive valuable traffic to your stand and use them as an extension of your sales team to funnel prospects.

Newbies – it might be your tenth expo of the year but don't forget how intimidating it was when you first wandered into the cavernous ExCeL (or equivalent). You may work in a giant industry but don't forget the friendliness that made it great to start with.

Opportunities – Careers are transitional, even more so in gaming and as much as we all like the idea of working our way to the top of one firm, statistically you'll be changing job sometime within the next three years. If you're looking for a change, there is no better place to research and meet with your future employer than a trade show, so take advantage of having them all within 500 feet of you.

Plan in advance - pick a building company who is already constructing stands at the conference and have it written in the contract that everything will be ready by 4pm the day before the show starts.

Quotes – if someone in the press asks to interview or for a vox pop, go for it. The same goes for pre and post event feedback. It's good for the event's future development and its free PR for you. Plus, it never hurts to promote your own personal brand once in a while.

Respect – for competitors, for your staff, for the event organisers, for women in gaming, for the bin men clearing up your mess and for yourself. This is essential and unequivocal.

Shoes – back to the standing again, killer Louboutin's (or uncomfortable Brogues) are not your friend if your ankles fuse by day three.

Travel Light – avoid over packing and keep your airport queue time and shoulder strain to a minimum.

Understand your market – it's amazing how much better your conversion rate becomes when you've looked into the companies you're meeting. Even a ten-minute Google search can give you enough insights to show you understand where you could offer an invaluable service and will set you apart from the majority who seem to wing it. Differentiation and a targeted offering will significantly increase your closing rates.

Vitamins – Berocca, Vitamin B and Iron are your friends. Nurofen might be your best mate. Take them with you.

Wrapping Up – try and recycle as much of your stand as you can – these things don't come cheap and the amount of unnecessary wastage these conferences generate is shocking. Again, a decent stand builder will help with this if you put it into the original brief.

X-Factor – There's no magic bullet for a successful conference but if you set challenging but achievable sales targets, motivate you team (incentivise if necessary), and focus on quality rather than quantity of meetings then you'll be on the right track.

You – look after yourself – between international conferences and all the affiliate events, your body and soul can take a pounding to play within your means and manage your time realistically.

Zzzz – if your employers don't offer a day in lieu after a weekend conference, they should, but take a day off to recharge anyway. If you're the boss, look after your most valuable resources and give your team a day off in lieu. Most likely they've earned it.

Chapter 24

The Balance Of Good Vs. Evil

Why Amazon's success proves consumers are choosing easy over ethical

How much is too much?

A pint of Speedway Stout sold by The Craft Beer Co. in London costs £22.50 – that's too much.

Teenagers wearing Jimmy Choo Diamond trail stretch mesh trainers, retailing at a smidge under six hundred quid? That's too much.

Potty-mouthed Chef Gordon Ramsay booking generic ballad machine Ed Sheeran for his daughter's 18th for half a million quid? That's too much.

But the king of profligate wastage must be HMRC who only billed multimedia retailing behemoth Amazon £220 million in taxes on UK revenues of £10.9 billion in 2018 – a highly attractive rate of just over two percent. Too much of a good deal, surely?

Amazon is a marketing wunderkind. From humble origins as an online bookseller in 1994 to the global retail, media, and data empire it's become today, most households in the UK are at least occasional customers. Many are superusers.

What's not to love?

Need a job lot of new nappies? Sure – here's the cheapest price available and you can have it delivered to your door this afternoon. Plus, if you sign up to Prime, you'll not only get free delivery, but we'll also chuck in a bunch of TV shows and movies to boot.

This alone would have laid the foundations for a significant empire, but Amazon is a world leader in the more nefarious world of big data, too. Whilst Google might just collect, analyse, and sell on information about your behaviours, Amazon not only owns the advertising channels and retail shopfronts (both digital and real world – they bought Whole Foods in 2017) but all elements of the distribution pipeline in between. They effectively know what you're going to buy before you do and manipulate manufacturing, availability, logistics and pricing accordingly.

Amazon is omnipotent.

In 2014 they made their most balls-to-the-floor move yet. If anyone had suggested before then that consumers would allow an advertiser to listen in on their private conversations in order to sell to them more effectively, there would've been universal outrage.

But founder Jeff Bezos doesn't hire stupid people.

In a Trojan Horse move of such astounding arrogance it would've made Odysseus blush, they sold Alexa as a 'digital home assistant', making it sound like a beneficial lifestyle tool, rather than a bugging device. Such brazen chutzpah takes significant balls, but with annual revenues in the hundreds of billions they can certainly afford Y-Fronts big enough to cradle them.

The company employs just over 27,500 people in the UK (each of whom, one assumes, is paying more traditional amounts in income tax) and as such, employer taxes made up the highest proportion of Amazon's bill, closely followed by business rates and corporation tax.

When there's so much cash at stake, you're able to employ the best of the best in the tax advisory world. Finance for the business is therefore redirected via Amazon EU in Luxembourg, meaning revenues from its retail, warehouse and logistics arms are buried well away from the eyes of the general public. If they were an individual employee, it's safe to say they'd spend from here to eternity being audited but as the third biggest company in the world after Microsoft and Apple, their clandestine dealings are, oddly, legal.

And it gets worse.

In the USA, Amazon hasn't paid a penny in tax for the past two years – despite revenues of $232 Billion and profits of $11.2 Billion. This forgiving regime was implemented by President Trump's Republican Party (although it was partially embedded prior to his inauguration)

So, they're conniving bastards, sure enough, but they're certainly not criminals – just a very successful service provider offering terrific value to time-poor households. Which brings us back to the Amazon's consumers, who are ultimately (and, apparently, happily) paying for this absurd level of profiteering. In an era of supposedly woke consumerism in which corporate social responsibility, purpose and brand activism are apparently high on a shopper's agenda, the majority of us are gleefully (if covertly) one-clicking our casual shopping via Amazon, accepting unnecessarily over-boxed packaging every week, if not every day.

If there were any rainforest left in the actual Amazon, it would be weeping.

This insane and frankly dangerous obsession with immediacy in our current 'Now culture' and addiction to rafts of unnecessary consumer goods puts the environment firmly below retail therapy, price, and convenience in our collective priority lists.

So called 'meaningful marketing' – in which brands adopt a stance on a popular social issues - was meant to be on-trend but really, does the majority truly care? Or do they just want to be seen to be caring? Hashtag Activism is certainly thriving…

In July 2018 Amazon was valued at £730 Billion and in late 2021 it had topped out at over a Trillion Dollars, of which Bezos is a 16% shareholder. Thanks to Digital Dumping, the majority of its retail operations are in fact losing money, designed more to build brand advocacy and collect data, with 75% of Amazon's profit coming from cloud services. He's comfortably the richest person in the world and even after a £28.8 Billion divorce bill last summer he was still worth £113 Billion. Yet Jeff hasn't followed the lead set by other Billionaires Bill Gates and Warren Buffett in committing the bulk of his riches to a higher philanthropic purpose.

Between delivery vehicles, packaging, Kindle production and Whole Foods, Amazon said it emitted 44.4 million tonnes of CO2 last year. In response to employee action (as noted in the same CBC Report) Bezos has claimed the company will be carbon neutral by 2040, but refuses to say how it's going to get there. He also refused to cut links to the oil and gas industry nor cull campaign contributions to climate deniers.

As the 25th biggest landowner in the States, he could positively offset his company's epoch-defining carbon emissions by planting a few trees at least, following the recent lead set by YouTubers Mr. Beast and Mark Rober in their support for The Arbor Day Foundation. The Foundation is on a mission to get 100 million CO2-guzzling trees in the ground by 2020 at a Dollar a sapling. Mr. Bezos's US tax rebate last year alone would plant 3 billion new trees, enough to repopulate the entire rainforest after which his company is named, and yet he seemingly remains on a single-minded track to self-fulfilment.

If he doesn't have a vault in one of his castles full of gold coins to dive into, I'd be sorely disappointed.

As Christmas approaches and panic shopping sets in, the streets will be paved by the detritus of Christmas future – millions of dampened Amazon boxes, their logo's ironic smirk grinning up from pavements around the world like a portentous Cheshire cat. The only

people that can curb Amazon's climb to global dominance (with associated negative impact on the planet) and put the environment back at the top of the public's agenda are the shoppers, who currently - behind closed doors, at least - don't seem to give a damn.

Chapter 25

Let's Get Ready To Rumble

Everything wrong with the £100 million Brexit ad campaign

One hundred million pounds buys you a lot of real estate in media land, as the British government has discovered with its current 'no deal readiness' ad campaign. A 2018 Nielsen report on UK advertising budgets suggests that Johnson's bulging purse would have placed Brexit as the fifth most profligate client in the UK's spending ranks after P&G, Sky, McDonalds and BT - the latter of whom spent £109.3 million on its UK advertising in 2018.

Next on the money train came programmatic monster Amazon with £87.5 million, Unilever, with a brand family that would make the benefit office wince at £82.8 million and in eighth spot, meerkat-toting insurance aggregators Compare the Market at £62.2 million.

But these tallies are *annual* spend figures. Brexit, in a spree reminiscent of a Kardashian with a tax rebate at the Harrods sale, is blowing its frankly unbelievable wad in a two-month period before the deadline on the 31st of October. Pro-rated through the whole of 2019, Brexit's annual spend would have been £600 million – enough for our illegitimately proroguing PM to 'sponsor' another sixty thousand of his resplendent chums.

According to the 2018 Advertising Association/ WARC Expenditure Report (which collects data from the entire media landscape) UK ad spend totalled £23.6 billion in 2018 - just under £65 million per day - so the Brexit campaign budget could, theoretically, have block-booked all the UK's advertising and media space, above and below the line, for a little over a day and a half.

All of it. Down to the last pixel, door drop and Tweet. Then at least this mad melee of Machiavellian mediocrity would've been over quickly.

According to turncoat Ewok Michael Gove, the Minister in charge of Brexit contingency planning "…ensuring an orderly Brexit is not only a matter of national importance, but a shared responsibility".

Presumably by 'shared responsibility' he was referring to the cost.

Gove referenced data suggesting that only 50% of the population believed it was likely the UK would actually leave the EU on 31st October, thus necessitating the inordinate levels of panic-spending on popular education via sub-par advertising.

The government backed his conviction that an exit was inevitable, deal or otherwise, by briefing a number of the great and the good in advertising to come up with an authoritative campaign to persuade the public that yes, this was happening. Get in shape and get on board or… or… well, just get on board. There's a good chap.

It should come as no surprise that although Alex Aitken, executive director of government communications is managing the campaign, the impetus and direction came from Gove, Johnson and his resident Iago Dominic Cummings, the puppeteer-in-chief behind the 'Vote Leave' campaign.

After a few abstentions, the Brexit campaign pitch was eventually won by New York headquartered Engine Group (whose parent organisations are Opinion Research Corporation of the New Jersey parish and Lake Capital out of Chicago). Media planning and buying, the lion's share of the cash pot, was pinched by Manning Gottlieb OMD, a subordinate brand of New York based OMD.

With all this talent and, one assumes at this price, every single creative resource at their disposal allocated to the brief, the client - the British public in this instance - would've deservedly expected a magnum opus of advertising genius to fill their flat screen TVs, laptops, tablets, mobiles, billboards, letter boxes and coffee mugs for the eight weeks up to November.

Perhaps an emotive, impactful, and effective masterpiece, redolent of Apple's epic 1984-inspired Superbowl commercial?

But no, not us unassuming, understated, placid, polite, ever-forgiving Brits. Those Mad Men decided that what we needed to spend our hard earned hundred million on was a patronising, simplistic Ronseal ad, art directed in PowerPoint, copywritten in fridge magnets and painted in ironically patriotic red, white, and blue.

It's so lightweight and prescribed you could almost hear the sound of a thousand palms hitting foreheads at creative agencies from Brighton to Belfast.

The campaign, currently rolling out on every possible media outlet 24/7, was initiated back in July with the government's syndicated brief entitled: - 'Prepare for Brexit'. Cleverly, New York's finest (with help from their London siblings, no doubt) decided they didn't need to reinvent the wheel so apparently visited Thesaurus.com, selecting literally the first recommended alternative - thus missing an obvious and rather more descriptive opportunity by rejecting 'Brace for Brexit' in what was presumably their one single, solitary and all too brief brainstorm.

The ads look like a National Express coach tipped on its bumper thus transcribed from landscape to portrait – subsequently, it's just not very good.

But then again, it is entirely on message. Simplistic, to the point, no sugar coating – what's the point in pretending this is anything it's not? As the saying goes, 'there's no way to polish a turd', and in this respect the agency is bang on message - their turd of a campaign remains unpolished.

Even if the billboards are naïve in their execution, you can't argue with their brevity. Eleven words, three colours, two numbers, an abbreviation and a link to the https://www.gov.uk/brexit website that leads confused Brits through an even more confusing questionnaire that supposedly fills in the gaps on what they should do if, as many suspect will be the case, no reasonable and feasible deal has been agreed by the end of next month.

Sadly, the most pragmatic suggestion "Run to Dover, wave goodbye to France, put your head between your legs and kiss your arse goodbye" appears to have been lost somewhere in the bowels of the website.

In such confusing times we should perhaps appreciate the direct nature of this creative approach and, given the significance of coming events, the blanket media coverage is a necessary, if ludicrously frivolous evil.

However, the enduring sentiment is one of continued disappointment, not that Brexit is happening – that's something inevitable decreed by formal and correct democratic process – just that our retreat out of the EU is being managed and communicated with all the panache, efficiency and potential longevity of a drunken Tinder hook up.

It doesn't bode well, does it?

We're in this together and the 'Get Ready for Brexit' campaign with its associated spend could and should have been handled much, much better.

Chapter 26

Generation A To Zzzz

How to communicate with teenagers without boring them to death

Fractured skull fragments hewn from a rock on the Mani peninsula in the Greek Peloponnese are, it's been claimed, the oldest Home Sapiens fossils ever found outside Africa.

The jigsaw of cranial bits and pieces is supposedly over 200,000 years old, meaning the skull has rewritten known history – it would be older than the previous record-holding *Homo sapiens* fossil found outside Africa by more than 160,000 years.

The baffling thing here is that we may now have over 150,000 years of uncharted interaction between Home Sapiens, our upstanding 'intelligent' forebears and Neanderthals - our stockier, shorter legged and now very extinct cousins.

Those seeking a thoroughly engaging analysis of what this means for human history should envelope themselves in the excellent book 'Sapiens' by Yuval Noah Harari. For those who fear being sunk by the tome's 512 pages, I can save you some time – Homo Sapiens and Neanderthal species were about as familial as the modern-day adult and their erstwhile teenage progeny.

Now I'm not suggesting for one second that the youngsters in this analogy are knuckle dragging thugs. In fact, evidence from my last visit to a Premiership football match suggests that adults can behave atrociously in the wrong circumstances, however there are undeniable and notable differences in the behaviours, attitudes, motivations, beliefs, desires, demeanour, and communications methodologies of those aged between thirteen and nineteen and the Gen X segment aged 40+ that set them poles apart.

These differences are as defined as they are longstanding and has meant that interaction between adults and teenagers has always been a tricky conundrum.

In the marketing world, audiences that have value to brands tend to earn their own title. For young people, their custom is so desirous we gave them two: -

Generation Y (AKA 'Millennials') are currently between 25 and 39 years old and have outgrown the trappings of teenage angst only to find themselves drowning in debt.

Then there's the current youth crop known as Generation Z - the newest tranche currently aged between 4-24 years old. To add context, this 'Z list' makes up 25% of the world's population and as such shouldn't be treated lightly - in the U.S. alone there are nearly 74 million of them, enough to make any Gen X marketer reach for their skateboard in a tragic and ultimately doomed effort to get down with da kids.

According to research by online bank Kasasa, the average Gen Z human receives their first mobile phone aged 10.3 years, grew up in a hyper-connected world and on average, spends at least three hours a day on some kind of mobile device. Notoriously cynical and rather unsurprisingly untrusting of their Gen X forebears (they are their parents, after all) communicating with these teenagers is a minefield, leaving in its wake a cemetery of misplaced adverts, ill-judged products and cynically rejected politics.

It should be no shock to anyone in marketing and advertising that teenagers think we're dicks.

According to Kat Krieger from coffee brand Joyride: - "…authenticity may have been a buzzword years ago, but this goes way beyond that […] younger generations are more aware and politically astute than ever before. […] marketing speak just won't cut it anymore. Consumers want quality, but they also want brands with integrity".

In addition to Krieger's unequivocal assertion in a 2018 report by Forbes, the following checklist is a good starting point if you want to earn trust and gain integrity with the Gen Z consumers:-

1.   Earn their attention - Generation Z is known as the social generation and you need to cut through billions of bytes of trash before you can even think of capturing their interest.

2.   Tell the truth – counterintuitively to our marketing tutelage, brands that speak plain truth are achieving cut through faster

3.   Work with influencers - but be aware of how easy it is to burn money and integrity when this (frequently) goes wrong (plus nearly 10% of Instagram accounts are Bots according to several reports)

4.   Treat them as individuals - 25% of the world's population plugged into social media means that they are fervently and constantly trying to express their individuality, so true personalisation should be the norm rather than the exception.

5.   Practice what you preach – you're speaking with digital natives who smell bullshit like you sniff a decent Pinot Noir. Define your positioning, make sure it resonates and plant it as a rock-solid foundation to every campaign or communication you send out.

6.   Focus on brand values - having brand integrity, humility and purpose is no longer desirous but absolutely essential.

7.   Admit you don't know anything – this should be the start of pretty much any brief assessment anyway, but it's always worth a reminder.

Media wise, we know mobile devices are the first port of call for Gen Z so it stands to reason that your content should be designed to sit comfortably on these devices (very comfortably – see points 1, 5 and 6 above). As a kick start, these are the big four destinations commanding attention from their eyes, ears, and fingers: -

Social Media – Instagram, Snapchat, Twitter and TikTok, Tencent's QQ/ WeChat and Sina's Weibo in Asia and VK in Russia to name a few front runners. That said, despite Facebook's best efforts to become the social channel for old people, it remains the world's favourite across the board

Streamed Video – Google's YouTube remains the king but don't discount other young upstarts, most notably the Amazon owned Twitch, a favourite of the esports community on which over 350 billion minutes of streamed content has been viewed this year alone.

Music – Apple, Amazon and Google still have their claws deeply embedded in the music scene but smaller, more niche Apps and video streaming services have significant numbers of loyal Gen Z tribes amongst their followers.

Esports - In a recent study 'From Nerdy to Norm: Gen Z Connects Via Gaming' conducted by Whistle, 91% of Gen Z males regularly play video games, only incrementally higher than Millennials (84%). Among both generations, the stereotype of gamers has eroded. 'Gamer' no longer conjures the negative affiliation of a lazy guy (or, as is often forgotten, girl) in their parents' basement but rather playing (and crucially watching) esports – it's seen as an essential social interaction.

Gen Z is a misleading, buzz-phrase term – a chuck away line much better expressed as simply 'young people'. They exist in huge volumes, they're fed up with their circumstances - socially, environmentally, and financially - and they actively challenge the patronising way in which they're currently marketed to. In the same way that many Gen X'ers would reject a pro-Brexit rant from a far-right 70-year-old UKIP member,

Gen Z have their own opinions and have an expansive and eminently sharable means of expressing them.

In evolutionary terms, it's all semantic anyway. In twenty years', time Gen Z will be marketing leaders and we'll be irrational and outdated crones howling at the moon. How we communicate with and market to this generation now will influence not only the world they'll live in but also how they'll act when they get into our shoes.

Generationally, they are the surviving sapiens leaving us, Gen X and upwards, as the shallow-browed Neanderthals facing inevitable extinction. In 200 Millenia our outdated tactics, strategies and campaigns might be dug up as digital relics to be analysed, discussed, and quickly derided as outdated fossils of a lost species.

Chapter 27

When Marketing Piggybacks On Sport

For every Nike "Write the Future" ad, there's a Head & Shoulders turkey with Joe Hart and a whole lot of stereotypical rubbish that surface around every big sporting spectacles

Every four years a glut of highly paid professionals gather together to unite the world, hammer their opposition, and prove to everyone that their team is number one. These teams are ad agencies, and their tournament will be well underway by the time Russia has kicked a ball in the general direction of Saudi Arabia on the 14th of June.

The World Cup is Adland's Valhalla – a heaven of high fees, even bigger media spends and lofty aspirations of greatness. Like their pig skin plundering counterparts in the field, history is littered with the corpses of the nearly men, lying prostrate at the feet of the gods.

For every Pele, there is something as stunning as Nike's "Write the Future" campaign. And then you'll stumble over the clawing corpse of Joe Hart, erstwhile England keeper. He not only fumbled a Head & Shoulders ad in 2014 but he palmed a Doritos campaign in the general direction of the net and was nutmegged by a Vauxhall car spot, too. Poor Joe.

The cream and the drivel

But all is not lost in a World Cup year. He might yet be offered a Pepsi contract – and they can save anything, even their terminal second place to their cola giant rivals. You'll struggle find anything as wonderfully uplifting (and baffling) as the Pepsi "Oktoberfest" ad from Germany 2006.

As with everything in life, however, the cream floats to the top leaving a murky curd of ill-conceived advertising drivel in its wake. Twin that with irrational media spends, shareholder pressure and a general hype vacuum of over exuberance and you've got what amounts to an advertising tournament being played in tandem with some errant ball dribbling.

Bad World Cup ads are as predictable as a Gary Neville platitude, so to help you spot the dogs from the diamonds, here's what's likely to be turning up for that landmark of human rights sports-washing, the Qatar 2023 World Cup: -

The Classico

Being realistic, the hallmark ads will come from the stable of Nike or Adidas. They spend big and they spend well and being actual sports brands they can legitimately feature the greats of the current game without looking desperate. Nike will likely feature the hairier Ronaldo, the greatest player in history (over 5 foot 8) doing something epic while resembling a slightly concerned Action Man. Adidas, meanwhile, will probably go for a moodier, team-based effort. Both will be brilliant, both will win awards and plaudits, neither will be anything we haven't seen before. They're almost clichés in their own greatness with "rinse and repeat every four years" instructions on the label, but I suppose if it ain't broke…

The Tone Deaf

A lot has happened since the last World Cup in Brazil. Globally, women's rights have been rightfully (if very belatedly) high on the agenda, latterly manifested through the #MeToo movement and it seems likely that this social media friendly hashtag will unfortunately prompt at least a couple of brands to leap on the feminist bandwagon.

It's a tricky issue to support legitimately through advertising and unless your brand positioning is appropriate, it'll likely end in teeth-sucking failure. That doesn't mean some brands won't give it a go, so expect women's football teams doing something empowering while fuelled by something powerful.

If anything, the inevitable backlash should be a fairly impressive firestorm to witness.

The 'Designed by Committee'

You know the one – all the money in the world and that's the best they could come up with. It's usually Ford or Hyundai/Kia - but at least they have the stones to back the game in the off season.

For any other car brand with a World Cup ad it's going to be business as usual. High production values, little or no engaging story and a football or stadium image slapped onto the background in post. Turgid, dull, and irrelevant - but being car ads they'll be no worse than the putrid crap we have to sit through for the other 3.9 years in the cycle.

The Official Sponsor

FIFA's <u>brand protection guidelines</u> are a wonder to behold.

Those guys take IP pretty seriously, meaning those that hand over the requisite coin to become Official FIFA™ WORLD CUP® Partners™ Russia 2018© can at least relax in the knowledge that FIFA will protect their interests, Sadly, the big global players such as McDonalds, VISA, Hyundai/Kia Motors, and Gazprom (I know, right?!) spank all their cash on the rights - leaving precious little space for any actual creative advertising. Expect big logos, big stars and big headlines featuring the words the rest of us aren't allowed to use™ - and very little else.

The Budweiser

"Yee Haaa British kin folk! It's World Series Cup time." Bud is backing up its long-term hugely under-appreciated support of the beautiful game (if not the beautiful planet) with eight million beer cups that light up when they hear a noise. So far, so Bud. Promoted via a drone invasion ad, this is just pure cash cow hyperbole, but kind of wonderful in its own "devil may care" way.

Bud has laid out its stall – they are the beer of soccer ball. Where others are just "probably", Bud is definitely "the King of beer soccer spenders" - and in 2018 they want everyone to know it.

The Gambling Ad

I ought to be careful here as this is my industry for the past 16 years, however it's such a rich seam of crapidity I simply can't ignore them.

All World Cup gambling ads are the same.

Seriously, even with a cursory look, they are.

The Engerland

My perennial favourite – the brave marketing folks nurturing UK brands who, despite significant evidence to the contrary, still think that one day we'll recapture the magic of '66. Think Carling, think Vauxhall, think M&S. When Gareth and his lads inevitably spoon a back pass into their own net against Belgium, thus ending our nation's chances for another four years, who'll be there to pick up the pieces? Who will count the advertising cost of a team that is already on the morose flight to Gatwick?

When Engerland came home before the postcards (©Guy Wootton, circa 1994) who will support the supporters? The glass is half full, absurdly optimistic marketers, that's who - they are the tournament's true MVPs.

All that spend and with absolutely zero chance of ever seeing a successful return – that's the measure of a truly legitimate England fan – and a big sports event campaign.

Chapter 28

Is This Really The Best A Man Can Get?

The real problems with Gillette's 'We Believe' ad campaign

Unlike many of its critics, I actually watched Gillette's 'We Believe' ad before deciding it was shite. Whether it was designed as such I'm not so sure, but you can't argue with the noisy and universal debate (and significant global awareness) it generated.

By now, you've most likely heard about Gillette's effort to capitalise on the #MeToo movement with their new brand ad titled 'We Believe'. In it, they challenge Menkind to be the best that they can be by association with the blades that are supposedly the best a man can get.

The ad has prompted ridicule and even threats of embargo by thousands of men offended by the simplistic and even patronising way in which the ad pigeonholes our sex as a universally imbecilic, incapable of acting in a manner acceptable in the modern age. Conversely, others have praised a brand of Gillette's stature (and by association parent company P&G) for outing the outdated behaviours of men and challenging us testicle wielding sapiens to dump our historical whimsy and find our spiritual home in the modern age.

An early critique was Piers Morgan on Good Morning Britain, a man whose opinion I hold in such disdain that I automatically disagreed with his flabby-jowled derision before I'd even seen it. Realising that I was at risk of doing exactly what everyone else had done by making up my mind without reviewing a shred of evidence, I watched the ad to make up my own mind.

And by God – Morgan was right – it's catastrophically bad - but not for the knee jerk reasons every shouty Twitter critic is lambasting it for.

In the 1 minute 48 second full version, director Kim Gehrig of UK production house Somesuch takes a big bag of derogatory clichés and hurls them like errant darts in the general direction of the male razor buying public in an effort to shame us, collectively and unequivocally, into changing the bad things that we as a sex are all, every one of us, apparently guilty of.

It's entirely irrelevant that Gehrig is a woman – she's a proven talent with a showreel of influential, empowering, and wonderful advertising that includes 'This Girl Can' for Sport England and 'Viva La Vulva' for Libresse. She's earned her stripes in empowering advertising which is exactly why P&G hired her – to drag Gillette's tired brand out of the '80s and into the disruptive environment razors are sold in today.

P&G spent over $7.2 billion on marketing and advertising in 2017 with over a billion Dollars going to Gillette. This is a product vertical with an astronomical margin attached and until recently very little in the way of global competition. That said, P&G's shareholders demand incremental returns which new product innovations such as multiple blade facias and vibrating handles only go so far in satiating. In order to stay ahead of younger upstarts like Dollar Shave Club and Harry's, the Gillette brand needs to be omnipresent and, they've now realised, current – thus their 'brave' brand direction.

The ad was viewed over nine million times on Gillette's own You Tube channel in its first two days on air and ten times that on other news channels bleating about its toxic masculinity. If you remove any of the subjective opinion about its content and compare it to one of Gillette's saccharine mini-soap opera efforts of yesteryear, then it's nothing but an incomparable marketing success story that happens to have a contentious, even controversial effort at social justice at its heart.

In reality it was a trope-laden cocktail of ill-conceived and misdirected cliché, but so what? I dislike most advertising and if that affected my purchasing behaviour I'd starve in a week. You don't spend Gillette's level of money without some considerable due diligence. They knew what fuse they were lighting and gave Ms. Gehrig the matches. She knew she was blowing up the right bridge because a million dollars in focus groups told her so. Yes, it's brave to zag when others zig - it's also brave to accept your Oscar whilst taking a dump on stage - still not a particularly good idea though...

The worst accusation I can level at the ad is that's it's a pretty poor piece of cliché-riddled film making with stock video from a 1998 male clothing catalogue shoot - but as a piece of noise generating advertising, it's annoyingly brilliant. I still won't be buying their products but only because they're thirteen quid a pack, not because I'm irredeemably upset at their advertising.

Chapter 29

Ho, Ho, Woe

Advertisers spend the year bleeding the tear ducts of reindeer to present a schmaltzy smorgasbord of sycophantic cobblers at Christmas. Sometimes they get it right.

Somewhere in the middle Atlantic Ocean there's a strip of sand known as Pig Beach. This desolate, rocky shore is jagged and unwelcoming, thanks to a long-distant volcanic heritage, and if you try hard enough you can find it on the appropriately named Pig Beach on 'Inaccessible Island', twenty eight miles from the slightly more placid island of Tristan da Cunha, itself over 1,500 miles off the coast of South Africa.

If you're not a people person, Pig Beach is your nirvana. However, at this time of year even the local penguin population is unnervingly aware that they'll be hard pushed to avoid the plethora of turgid Christmas ads that everyone on the planet is traditionally subjected to.

No matter where you are, there is no escape from the advertiser's season of goodwill.

In advance of this annual maelstrom of commercial saccharine, here's what you can expect to hit the airwaves sometime after Bonfire night:

Let's begin with the fan's favourite – the much-loved retail establishment.

John Lewis (and their Partners, apparently) have owned the Christmas retail category over the past decade but everyone from Debenhams to ASOS have been buying in agencies, media and talent trying desperately to catch up and steal a little slice of the public's hearts.

For all the joy the John Lewis Christmas campaigns have spread over the years (Buster, Monty, From Me to You) – they've excelled themselves, to be fair), commercially, they're only just recovering from what can only be descried as the Marianas Trench of share price crashes, hitting a low of eighty pence on the 3rd of October.

That means they're under the cosh, which puts a horrific amount of pressure on their incumbent agency, advertising's Wunderkinds adam&eveDDB to deliver like Santa on crack.

But this should present no significant bother – this shit is totally formulaic. A&E DDB just need to inject a little extra Christmas sparkle to the formula to make it work and run it step by step:

- Animation? God yes – let's not risk alienating anyone with real life here - and if kids love it, then so do parents, right? Best go with Aardman – it's the only way to be sure
- Hollywood director – preferably an Oscar winner. And/ or a woman. Tick a diversity box if you can.
- Media spend – who do you want to reach? For this they have to heed the advice of Gary Oldman's wonderful character Stansfield in Leon. "Bring me everyone".

- Fairy Dust – this is the extra hidden gem – the unquantifiable magic that makes a good Christmas ad great. Problem is, John Lewis have had such an extraordinary a run of success that their wonderful campaigns are now as anticipated as a Katie Price meltdown in The Sun. If she's not available, then maybe an A.I. driven virtual reality version of Marilyn Monroe? Something – anything – is needed to fuel the zeitgeist.
- Music – an all-time heart-rending classic or an up and coming artist with a sob story and a moving melodic guitar tune? If in doubt, best to throw more money at the problem to guarantee success.

That means Elton. The Rocket Man.

Who they'd already signed up.

For five million quid.

For a sodding TV ad.

How many Le Creuset pans is that?

Back to planet normal and we can be reassured by our supermarket chains and their Christmas ad offerings. You can set your watch by the executions the big supermarkets trundle out year after year:

- Tesco – Big name (British) talent, endearingly cack-handed male & controlling, bubbly and empowered female. Thin plot line featuring several key Christmas dinner staples. Amusing but inoffensive sign off somewhere around the till.

- Sainsbury's – They think they're better than Tesco, and so do their customers so they'll have higher production values, more middle-class talent, and a homely setting in which the message is more subtle – Christmas is about family, love and giving. Nice.

- Waitrose – Posh and expensive – they know it, you know it. It's the same stuffing as Aldi's but it's made with crumbed focaccia by an artisanal baker called Francoise and costs eleven quid. Deal with it.

- ASDA – WHAT A HAPPY TIME! IT'S CHRISTMAS! ASDA staff, good pricing, no bullshit. I love ASDA. It knows it's a shop selling well priced food that's OK. That's it. You know what you're into here. If John Lewis tried this low production values/ focus on cost approach, the Royal Borough of Hammersmith & Chelsea would have an attack of the vapours. As it is, you expect a lot for a little, and you get exactly that.

- Morrisons/ CO-OP – Like Sainsbury's but with considerably less pricey talent. Kids will feature if for no other reason than they don't have hardnosed agents and can pull a cracker on demand.

- Lidl & Aldi – "Here's a fucking turkey. And some spuds. It's safe to eat and doesn't taste like your sock draw. Have a Christmas – or we'll send Kevin the Carrot round". Job done.

Back in la-la land, the wonderful people at 'Perfume Ads for Sale' (@PerfumeAds on Twitter) really should be reaping it in as we approach the festive period. Fragrance manufacturers wrote the book decades ago when it comes to seasonal bullshit in advertising.

It seems they traditionally spend 1% of their budget on strategic insight, 4% on cocaine and the remaining twenty million split evenly between media, a trending Hollywood star, and enough postproduction lens flare to make George Lucas nervous.

Perfume ads are astonishingly vapid at the best of times - but this year it'll get undoubtedly worse - we can expect a healthy dose of crow-barred #MeToo/ Diversity references that seem oddly ill-fitting next to Natalie Portman's soft focussed bottom.

But what do I know? They're the pros when it comes to selling smells (sorry, 'anticipatory essences') to desperate, witless husbands like me.

Toys – Two and a half words – 'Toys R Us'. Now, this paradise of kid's nonsense has gone belly up, who's going to educate us on what's hot and what's not in the child quietening world?

It's Amazon, that's who.

Those American retail bastards have got all of us by the short and curlies, haven't they? Cheaper, easier, and with a bit of ethical self-brainwashing, they're the geniuses who let us find, pay, wrap, and deliver all our gifts with a minimal amount of fuss (although apparently with the maximum amount of rainforest destroying packaging, it seems).

Amazon will advertise everything this Christmas, including toys, and it'll all be so fricking easy. My godchildren already have wish lists and my daughter has a nursery that may as well have an Amazon smiley logo decal stuck on the ceiling. It's all shits & giggles until they own the world, then we'll be made to pay.

Damn you and your easy, ruthless efficiency, Amazon. Damn you.

Charities – it must be bloody hard working at a charity. Flogging gadgets, clothes or food is easy by comparison. Christmas is inevitably a time in which charities need to collect the maximum amount in donations and yet not only is the media landscape hugely overcrowded with competitors but also the audience is broke. Those iPhone X's are over a grand and kids want a stocking, too.

But hold fire – these are the ones that matter, aren't they? No matter what your role in this dizzying industry, you're doing alright.

Others definitely aren't. The Guardian published a handy list of the top 1,000 UK charities here so next time you're about to splurge in response to an emotionally manipulative Christmas ad, why not pick one of the less trendy ones from the bottom of the list and give them some love? A donation or even volunteering a little of your time would be hugely impactful.

Save some of your professional, social, and monetary equity for those who can't buy an Alessi Stovetop Kettle with Melodic Whistle for one hundred and seventy-two quid.

There are plenty of people out there who won't even see the John Lewis ad selling it in the first place.

I

Chapter 30

New Tech For Old Problems And How To Keep Up With The Disruptors

Can marketing innovate alongside era-defining brands?

It's getting to the point where no tech company feels it can be taken seriously unless it's disrupting something. Anything. Just finding an old problem and solving it with a simple, intuitive solution.

This new-fangled trend for exposing the limitations of an industry by inventing a solution through the use of technology, and rapidly dominating it until a multibillion-dollar IPO, is all we read about in the pop-up blogs of TechCrunch, *Forbes,* and LinkedIn.

And it's great – really it is. Even for this wizened hack of a marketer (who spurns Apple products as plug-in jewellery for tweens and can't work a satnav).

We marketing types are normally quite handy when it comes to adopting innovation: PPC, the commercialisation of social media, helicopter banners and the T-shirt cannon, to name but a few random examples. However, with this recent glut of disruptive firms dominating the headlines (and yes, Airbnb, Uber, Salesforce, Snapchat, Deliveroo – this includes

269

the likes of you lot and your clever workforces), the marketing industry has yet to act as the innovator-in-chief when it comes to marketing tactics, strategies, and attribution.

Steps toward successful disruption can be loosely outlined as follows:

1. Find a sector that has high revenue yield, low barriers to entry and is dominated by a limited number of low-tech suppliers.
2. Come up with a consumer solution that delivers a product or service to your chosen segment's consumers at lower cost, with less hassle or in less time (preferably all three). It will also help to iron out any bugs or potential sticking points before going to market, something more easily achieved by looking at where early adopter businesses in the sector have come a cropper.
3. Deliver this solution through a free app or website and market the bejesus out of it. Celebrity aficionados and a viral/ UGC (see glossary) element certainly won't harm your chances.

If we use the three steps suggested above and overlay them onto marketing channels (which in turn will act as the 'sectors' in point 1), it might allow the marketing industry to catch up with the disruptive firms and become thought leaders, rather than service providers.

We'll start with a big one – as far as many marketing budgets go, at least:

ATL advertising

Currently advertising comes in two packages – brand and direct response. Both require creative, a media plan/buy and measurement KPIs (plus the capability to actually measure success – more of that shortly). But what if traditional TV media was planned and purchased in the same way as PPC (pay-per-click)? You'd have a more accountable spend (which finance directors like) and more targeted advertising (which consumers like) leading to less wastage and a more efficient spend.

"But how the hell would that work?" I hear you splutter into your lattes.

That's the thing – with the current tools, reliance on agency analytics management and data availability from Sky, ITV, and the like, it can't be done. But imagine if you disrupted this model – say by tapping into real-time viewing analytics from the proliferation of 4G TVs and a real-time bidding platform, so your media team could buy and place ads (and then optimise them) with pinpoint accuracy to hit the most ideal consumer segments? There would still be wastage, for sure, but it would be significantly less than the current state of affairs, and attribution/success measurement would be done in real-time – which would facilitate even more effective digital spending.

Online and social display

No one said disruptive ideas had to be wholly original – in fact, the very way in which Uber has grown to be a phenomenal success owes as much to late-night cab firms as it does to its booking interface. So, looking at one of the major flaws in regular online display, you'll see that most ads are ignored. This is, after all, a high-volume, low-return channel in which a 5% click rate is hailed a breath-taking success in some industries. Which makes you wonder, how have other disruptors made content more appealing?

Like eBay...

If consumers saw a skyscraper, MPU or page takeover that gave them the opportunity to bid the price or offer they'd be willing to go to for the item in question, it's a tautology that click rates (and sales) would go up. Now, you'd need to work out what price you're prepared to suffer to ensure the sale remains commercially viable, so maybe you offer a selection of promotional deals instead? Tailored, time-sensitive, consumer-generated pricing. Sure, there are holes as big as Elon Musk's garage in that one, but it's different, customer-centric, and value-driven – so there's potential.

PPC

PPC analysis has become as ubiquitous to marketing meetings as dodgy biscuits and brown loafers. Google's search behemoth is not only accountable, but even the most technophobic marketing director can log into their AdWords and GA accounts and see their spend in action.

The most recent disruptive technology in PPC is programmatic advertising, where big brands (with independent trading platforms like

Xaxis and Rocket Fuel) and agencies (such as Essence and MediaCom) can create automated bidding strategies for keywords.

Sensory marketing

To date, reading and listening have been the greediest senses as far as marketing goes. But that's ignored touch, taste, and smell. Now there's a very good reason for this – the analogue and latterly digital space doesn't have the capability to disseminate smells, flavours, or touchable experiences. However, the introduction of the home 3D printer will allow consumers to touch product shapes at home – and as for smell and taste, just imagine what you could achieve with those.

From washing powder manufacturers to vintners, Ben & Jerry's to Ann Summers, consumers would have an incredible interaction with products in three or even four dimensions before deciding to purchase.

If you're looking for inspiration about the capabilities of sensory marketing, get to the <u>Tate Sensorium</u>, an immersive display featuring four paintings to stimulate your senses showing until 20 September at Tate Britain.

Online video

YouTube is, oddly, the second-biggest search engine in the UK, but its ad platform remains wedded to Google's bidding protocols. However, this status quo is ripe for disruption. In fact, the opportunity to empower a media-owner's content is already in hand via companies like Grabyo, which allows rights-holders to capture bite-sized clips from any live video feed and share them instantly across social platforms complete with ads and links from sponsors.

"The viral nature of social video, particularly real-time video from premium sports or music-rights holders, means that sponsors can reach tens of millions of consumers from a single clip without any paid media buy," says Gareth Capon, chief executive of Grabyo. "Brands are enjoying engagement on a scale that was previously unavailable outside of television."

Mobile and apps

The tablet and mobile revolution is nearing climax and getting eyeballs on your offering in these tiny pieces of real estate has become even more challenging. So how far are we from a tipping point for advertisers in which supplying a free smartphone to consumers in exchange for their loyalty becomes a commercially viable decision?

If Tesco could, for example, have a contractual guarantee that a family of five would do its weekly shop with Tesco Online for the next three years, what would that be worth? An iPhone? A smart TV? Lease payments on a family car? I strongly suspect that affiliate extensions into a micro-affiliate sphere (taking cashback models to the next level) will be the norm within the next year or so.

So will all this happen? Certainly not exactly as described above, or I'd be expecting Sir Martin Sorrell on my doorstep with a bouquet of flowers and an offer letter. But what is certain is that the marketing world is no different a commercial animal than any other industry, and if you find a tech solution to an old problem that makes things simpler, easier, cheaper, and more effective, then you should go ahead and do it – you'll be onto a winner.

After all, Airbnb is really nothing more than a lettings agency with a dating site algorithm at its core and good backing, isn't it? How hard can it be?

Chapter 31

Playing The Game

In football, as in marketing, you ignore the rules at your peril

The introduction of VAR into professional football (soccer to American readers), is now seen on reflection to be largely beneficial to the beautiful game rather than a hindrance and has made the chancers in football a little more honest. What was at risk of being debased into a game of bluff and bluster now has a chance of redeeming its status as 'the beautiful game'.

However rules in any part of life have the opportunity to be interpreted and, if possible, loopholes found. Referees are human, players are well versed in gaming miniscule illegitimacies to win an edge and the world most costly player, Brazil's Neymar, is fast becoming a parody of himself with his histrionics as he tries to break the somersault world record at every opportunity, his misguided aim being to win through the provision of free kicks and penalties at all times.

For us gambling marketers, our rules are not overseen by a bank of cameras and a team of secondary referees but there are officials whose job is to ensure we stay within the boundaries of fair play. These authorities are the Advertising Standards Authority with their CAP and BCAP codes of practice and the UK Gambling Commission. These august bodies don't need cameras and replays as gaming marketing campaigns are designed by their very definition to be highly visible to as many people as possible.

Footballers may feign a trip – we on the other hand are telegraphing our mistakes on the biggest stage we can afford.

On the 28th of June the Gambling Commission published a report that included a statement from the Chief Executive Neil McArthur covering the following key areas of their compliance focus.

- Anti-Money Laundering
- Customer Interaction
- Self-Exclusion
- Unfair Terms and Practices
- Advertising and Marketing
- Illegal Gambling

The goalposts have been moved to protect consumers, the wider public and raise standards in the industry with the added benefit of improving the integrity of the gaming industry. The fines associated with non-compliance are becoming scary in their scale and frequency.

These dodgy players aren't U.S. facing Costa Rican licensed sportsbooks either. Check out this list of big-name brands (this is a highlight reel – there are plenty more) and subsequent fines and have a think:

·   **William Hill** - £6.2m penalty package for social responsibility and money laundering failures.

- **Leo Vegas -** £600,000 penalty package for advertising breaches

- **888** - £7.8 million penalty package for failings in handling vulnerable customers.

- **Skybet** - £1 million fine for failing to protect vulnerable consumers

Do you act more in line with the rules than these hallmark brands? Are you sure? Look at those numbers and have then decide if a full audit of your campaigns and operating protocols doesn't sound like a pretty sensible idea. You can start by reading the ASA's updated CAP and BCAP Codes.

The Gambling Commission will continue to set and enforce standards that the industry must comply with to protect consumers.

In all of the sections, there are examples of enforcement action undertaken, details of the financial penalties imposed and a "health check" for each area advising on what you can employ as best practice on the topics covered.

There is no interpretation of the rules – these are the rules. Those operators that don't comply are going to find that eventually there will be a price to be paid that'll hurt much more than an exit in the quarter finals of the World Cup.

Chapter 32

Hubble, Bubble, Toil & Trouble

What the past could teach us about the future of Cryptocurrency

(Originally written in 2017 – so some values are *hopelessly* out of date…)

"I'm forever blowing bubbles, pretty bubbles in the air,

They fly so high, nearly reach the sky,

Then like my dreams they fade and die".

I'm Forever Blowing Bubbles, Kendis, Brockman & Vincent, 1919

Leading Cryptocurrency Bitcoin has recently passed the once dreamt-of benchmark of a $6,000 market valuation *($67k in November 2021 – who knew, eh?!)*. This astounding figure is set to increase further still, with some (mainly those 'With Bitcoin') suggesting it could even have the capacity to reach a stratospheric $100,000 and beyond. For cynics, a group comprised in significant number by those 'Without Bitcoin', the lunacy of excitable investment has long since pushed the perceived value passed its peak.

One could imagine those that missed the boat may even hold informal celebrations of schadenfreude when the bubble eventually pops.

In recent history we've been witness to a number of similar extravagant investment frenzies. The one that sticks in my mind was the Dot Com boom. As a twenty-two-year-old in my first paid job I didn't have the money to invest in Boo.com, Lastminute and their ilk - so I invented Google instead.

OK, so that's not strictly true. My 'FindMy.com' search engine concept came a year after Google launched and my friend Guy and I had no coding, marketing, or business experience whatsoever. Instead, we bought domains - lots of them - when they cost a salary busting twenty-six quid a pop.

Adding to our own ignominy, in our wisdom we whacked a sodding hyphen into all the 'Find-my' domains making them, if indeed it was possible, even more worthless. They say you learn from expensive mistakes, but if that were true, the two of us would have graduated from Mensa that year, instead of taking a two grand bath.

If our dot com bubble experience did teach me anything, it was that in no single instance can everybody profit from one scenario. For some to win, others must inevitably lose. Cryptocurrency is doing a damn good job of proving that theory right now, and it's just the latest in a long line of excitable bubbles to make heroes of the few and paupers of the masses.

Looking back further than my own bubble popping experience, the Dutch Tulip Mania of the 1630s was the first instance in which collective investment hysteria and groupthink pushed the value of a commodity to a ceiling far beyond any actual worth. In this Golden Age of tulip bulbs (the floral innovatory wunderkind of their time) prices for some bulbs of new and trendy tulips reached absurdly high levels. It wasn't to last, and according to Investopedia, "…it all came to an end in 1637, when prices dropped, and panic selling began. Bulbs were soon trading at a fraction of what they once had, leaving many people in financial ruin".

On the surface, cynics and some experts alike find the tulip boom 'rise and wilt' to be a like for like comparison to what Bitcoin and the Cryptocurrency movement is going through right now.

'The price activity and manic sentiment that led to present prices have dwarfed even the Tulip mania of nearly 400 years ago. The success of Bitcoin has spawned 800 plus clones (Altcoins) and counting, most of which are high-tech, pump-and-dump schemes. Nevertheless, investors have eagerly bid them up." (Elliott Prechter, 13th July 2017).

However, this comparison might not be the most accurate historical lesson.

Peter Kroll, Inventor of the Bitcoin Paper Wallet at BitAddress.org has suggested a more pertinent point of reference:

"The South Seas Bubble is a better comparison. In that bubble the British government legislated a monopoly on fishing the South Seas which created distorted market opportunities and opened the door to fraudsters claiming they had been granted a government monopoly. Fraudsters are now cloning Bitcoin and making baseless claims preying on irrational exuberance. The Tulip Mania by comparison was about a perishable consumption product that was used by wealthy people to show-off to their neighbours. Tulips were never seen as an investment, although some traders lost money searching for rare Tulip bulbs".

Whilst tulips are pretty and the South Seas bubble promised fishy riches from a faraway land, the benefits of Cryptocurrency are much more tangible. Fluency of currency transaction and the removal of the banking world as our dark financial overlords are two key attractions of digital currency. Add to that the anonymous way in which it can be used to transact – useful for both legitimate and nefarious Dark Net purposes alike. You can start to see why there would be a need for Cryptocurrency, and wherever there is a need there soon follows value.

In the 1630s, the pace of tulip bulb value growth was hindered by the speed in which rumours could fly, hype could be inflated, and funds transferred. Now, it only takes twenty minutes to set up an account with any number of crypto brokers like the £100 Billion-valued Coinbase, Binance, eToro and Plus500 to name four monsters amongst hundreds.

It's not only a few digital coin brands, either. Most of you will have heard of Bitcoin, Ethereum, Doge and Ripple. But if those bandwagons are too far down the trail for you, then take your pick from the other 2,000 or so coins that have gone through an ICO (Initial Coin Offering, or Token Sale – best explained by Nasdaq). Launching new coins to market is a gold rush in the truest sense, and the fact that the list includes 'Big Boobs Coin' should give you a clue as to the legitimacy of some of the clowns driving the wagons.

New Coins are introduced every week, many focussed on one product or service - from the Internet of Things to Cycling, Peace to Porn. A significant percentage of coin founders (showing a lack of financial fraud awareness not seen since Bernie Madoff nurtured an interest in pyramids) are spamming the internet trying to drum up interest and investment in their Token Sales by fair means and foul. Most of these ICOs and subsequent Cryptocoins will come to nothing, but that's not stopped mass market punters from piling in.

Greed, Ad Hoc self-regulation, and lack of public understanding are an ugly cocktail and one which does nothing to shore up the near-term integrity of Cryptocurrency as a whole. That said, it does look as though Blockchain currency is here to stay, in some guise at least.

Within this mire of uncertainty, it's difficult for experts (let alone the amateur investor) to really understand what they're buying into. What is the actual hard value of Cryptocurrency? According to Kroll, "…Bitcoin is backed by electricity. Its base value is the electrical cost to mine a coin. The expenditure of electricity to create Bitcoin is also what solves the double-spending problem and secures its most important feature - irreversible payments. Additionally, there is utility value from transactional demand for Bitcoin to digitally transfer value peer-to-peer on the Internet without the permission of intermediaries".

The industry I work in, online gambling, tends to be at the forefront of new tech innovation and has adopted the new currencies with a fervour. Beyond simple transactions there have been a glut of new gaming entities springing up that only utilise Bitcoin, and they appear to be gaining at least some traction.

People, especially in the media, like dealing in absolutes, marvels, and disasters. I won't be perverse by making personal (useless) predictions but perhaps a few notes of caution against popular perception to your potential investors is a fair compromise:

· Cryptocurrency exists and doesn't appear to be going anywhere soon – true

· It will keep growing in value forever – false – there are only so many people in the world who can invest at ever increasing valuations

· It's likely to crash soon – also false – it could continue to rise or perhaps stabilise like any currency, the London property market, or the price of a Snickers bar.

· There's still time to invest and make a killing – possibly, but also possibly not. As with any uncertain speculation, only bet what you can afford to lose

· Newer Coins might make more money if I get in early at their Token offering. Maybe, but do you remember Pets.com? Exactly...

Future prediction is a dangerous game, historical analysis the only feasible alternative. The problem is, there is no relative scenario in history with which we can compare the rise of Cryptocurrency. Add to that numerous misconceptions in what it does, how it works and the perceived 'get rich quick' opportunity and you end up with a fragmented mess of inconceivable data. The pipers who adopted early are motivated to sell the dream – they profit by over-hyping the future, thus potentially misleading the rats that follow them.

If we track the money trail to find an astute mentor to guide us through this unknown space, the name George Soros would be near the top of the pile. His perception is telling:

"Stock market bubbles don't grow out of thin air. They have a solid basis in reality, but reality as distorted by a misconception".

Defining your own sentient conclusions out of the muddle of Cryptocurrency misconceptions is the investor's sole challenge. What looks on the surface like easy money most certainly is not. Or it is... what's certain is no one knows anything with any degree of certainty.

For now, Bitcoin's value keeps rising and many lucky speculators have made Cloud-based fortunes. They are, however, still living in a gold-plated bubble and only get the key to the treasure chest when they decide cash out.

Chapter 33

The Game Of Life & How Commerce Is Influenced By Play

There are more similarities between gaming and marketing than you might realise as brands tap into the human desire 'to win'.

Choose 'sounds', press 19, 65, 9, then 17 and you'll hear a chime. Hold 'B' and press 'Start' then hold 'X' and press 'Start'.

This is the cheat code to choose any level on the Sonic the Hedgehog 2 game. Press a few buttons and a whole new universe opens up to you. If only marketing were so straightforward...

It's all about buttons and keys. People enjoy the challenge to their dexterity and the risk/ reward payoff of a game while the computer does the hard work behind the scenes. Funnily enough, our relationships with commerce, product development and marketing are going much the same way.

Why? Games are fun. Playing is fun. Playing a game and winning brings a warm, empowering feeling of success. And people like that feeling.

When we're trying to sell something, we often talk about creating emotional bonds, meaningful relationships, and positive vibes. All these things happen when someone feels that they're winning.

In sales strategy, many standard methodologies can be related to a winning feeling – price anchoring, scratch cards, even the Weber-Fechner law related particularly to price reductions for products and services. The law hypothesises that a saving of approximately 10% is the average point where customers are moved to action – to make the purchase. This is therefore the time when the majority feel they are winning.

In campaign terms, 'play' and 'win' are terms that litter the campaign review pages of this very publication every week. Brands have taken this even further within their product marketing, my favourite recent example being Doritos with its Doritos Roulette product. Its claim that in every handful you run the risk of eating a Tabasco flavoured chip is enough to make Christopher Walken wince.

It looks like you can now turn anything into a game.

Employing the notion of playing a game therefore enhancing your 'win' is a long-standing loyalty and retention device too. For the past 30 years McDonald's has famously and successfully recycled its Monopoly promotion – and the numbers are undoubtedly significant.

Sales promotion as a channel almost exclusively employs game devices – BOGOF, scratch & win, mystery prize, lucky dip – think of a fun fair game and chances are it's been utilised by brands at one time or other.

The game mechanics are getting tired – but that's no reason for consumers to change their behaviour. Marketers need to find new and exciting ways to gamify their sales funnels and conversion pipelines. One obvious innovatory port of call is the world of computer and mobile games.

Beyond the channel marketing mechanics, game play is also how we frequently oversee product creation, marketing, and distribution. The concept of push button manipulation is also now commonplace in the way we track, evaluate, and optimise not only campaigns but product production too.

The world of commerce is becoming increasingly game-like with people handling the controls.

Don't believe me? Let's have a look at the trending tools of the day. From the birth of a product (let's use a pair of sunglasses as an example) until it arrives in the hands of a consumer the world of commerce is becoming increasingly game-like with people handling the controls in the form of a keyboard and a mouse.

A.I. – through artificial intelligence, manufacturers are enabled with one button to scope out the global market for sunglasses, track current and future trends, source materials and design its first pair of 'Ray Bots'. The computer needs switching on and programming, in the short term at least, and human oversight to make sure your laptop hasn't self-actualised and renamed itself Cyberdyne Systems while you've been making a cup of tea.

You, the manipulator can sit back and watch the product take shape.

3D printing – you (or more likely in the future the AI programme you developed) feeds in a CAD drawing. Already eyewear manufacturer Mykita uses 3D printing technology for its Mylon collection. The company started working with polyamides as far back as 2007 using SLS (Selective Laser Sintering).

Marketing – This part of the game is computer driven already. Programmatic and automatic attribution modelling defines marketing strategy and spending for a great proportion of the FTSE 100.

Distribution – Your weekly grocery shop online is already using machine learning to forecast behaviour through trends to predict repeat grocery orders, which can be smart enough to adapt to your behaviour. Plugged into your calendar it can even adapt to your habits. The mother of machine learning for sales and distribution is Amazon. The Bezos behemoth tends to be pretty good at such things and already knows more about your buying preferences than you ever will. In fact, I'd be very surprised if they didn't already have an algorithm in testing that knew your future purchasing to such a degree of certainty that it could charge your card, mail out the products you need and wait for you to return anything you didn't want. And the return percentage would be nominal, too. Plus, drones.

Evaluation – From Facebook to Feefo, everything and anything can be evaluated and reviewed in seconds. It doesn't take a great leap of imagination to plug this feedback back into the original AI network and update the product dimensions, colour, or volume accordingly. By this stage you barely need to press the buttons – the game is playing itself.

What started as fun is now embedded in not only our social behaviours but also the methods with which the business world creates dollars from raw materials. The intuitive design of game play, the human nature around the desire to win and the shared parallels between playing a game and manipulating tools, machines and people have blurred the lines between what was once fun and what is now serious business.

This game is getting out of hand – and if the machines get much more advanced then you and I might end up being surplus to requirements.

Game over. You lose. Thanks for playing.

Chapter 34

You Can't Ditch Brand For Performance Marketing – Even In Digital

It's difficult to create true differentiation today, but even in online-only industries you still need brand marketing to make performance marketing effective.

Panini football stickers – a great product, no doubt about it. No skill required, inherently social and with a low barrier to entry. They were the ultimate in cheap, disposable, and sharable media. A fantastic brand.

The yo-yo was also a winner. Everyone at school had one, and they could all master at least a few tricks. It was an egalitarian toy – almost Communist in its universal equitability. Duncan's yo-yos were the brand of choice for any discernible 'dog walker'. They were crucial.

Then skateboards came along – more expensive, harder to master and you had to spend every school breaktime for at least a term learning how to ollie. But whether you could pull off a backside heel flip or not, you had to be wearing the right shoes to try it – and those shoes were Vans.

Even as early as the 1970s, with the Sk8 Hi and Old Skool models, Vans were cool. But why were they cool? Their aura was part rugged product and part California skate mystique. The pros wore them, according to everyone in the break after double maths. Tony Hawk rode in no other, apparently – and if they were good enough for Tony, well...

Vans were the archetypal trending brand, ultimately transcending a universe way beyond skating. Their perceived quality and desirability were more about the myth and legend that surrounded them than the rubber, leather and cotton that built them. This urban folklore added significant desirability value in the minds of a million knee-high skaters worldwide who pestered their parents and caused a sales spike only replicable by the spending power of sports shoe giants Nike and Adidas.

Brand awareness, perception and advocacy make customer acquisition campaigns work more effectively.

A brand such as this – and its disciples Etnies, Airwalk and Vision Streetwear – owed a great deal of its sales success to the word-of-mouth narrative that surrounded it. The brand stories were the viral media of their day, thus replacing media spend with direct revenue.

Nowadays everything is a brand. Your fridge, sunglasses, car, pork pie, G&T. If the vapid, vacuous Bisto-hued cast of Love Island speak about themselves as 'brands' in the third person then something's gone seriously wrong, right?

As marketers our world is not only built with brands, but also defined by them. This means enhanced perception and differentiation is extremely difficult, especially in sectors such as automotive, grocery, beauty, technology, and beverages.

But in performance-driven industries such as the one I work in, online gaming, is it any different?

Whether you fancy a flutter or not, you might perceive gambling as a more value-driven pastime – choose your sport, select your market, find the best odds, decide on your stake comfort zone, and click 'bet now'. Marketing success is all about shortening the 'awareness to spend' path – so the key metrics are low cost acquisition, clinical conversion, optimised retention, and enhanced reactivation, leading to incrementally growing customer lifetime values. The same model can be overlaid onto most online businesses from flight booking to music streaming.

To some CFOs in gaming, costly brand marketing campaigns might look like vanity spending – even wastage.

However, if you look at the big success stories in online gaming – PokerStars, Mr. Green, Foxy Bingo, Unibet to name but a few – they all share one common thread. They invest in brand marketing as much as direct marketing every single year. The big chief, Bet365, is rumoured to spend north of a £400m per year on marketing worldwide, brand advertising and sponsorship being a significant proportion of that.

In simple terms, enhanced brand awareness, perception and advocacy make their 'nuts and bolts' pay-per-click, display, affiliate and other customer acquisition campaigns work more effectively, deliver customers for less money and ultimately increase their return on investment.

Out of the gambling success stories there are very few exceptions to this rule. The brand I work for, Pinnacle, is one of them. We differentiate on value and availability – taking less margin, meaning we offer better odds, and we don't restrict successful punters (you'd be amazed how common account blocking is). We are, however, unique in this positioning.

The gaming industry has always been a front runner in performance marketing – second only to adult entertainment, supposedly. There's a whole heap of money to be made and with that opportunity to constantly tap into a well of riches comes innovation.

There is no 'brand' versus 'direct' debate. Brand marketing itself can deliver customers, and direct campaigns can help build brands.

For any brands competing in a performance-driven environment, it seems you have two choices: differentiate on product and price to such an extent that you stand alone or find a balance between brand investment and direct response to generate interest, fill your customer funnel and convert the highest percentage possible.

From there, squeezing value from every customer is crucial, which is where gaming has once again been a front runner with the adoption and total integration of data science, big data and analytics (here's a handy guide of what each area stands for). The gaming industry, and more recently marketing as a whole across every sector, now lives and breathes through data-led decision making and daily use of tools like R.

Data is now unequivocally cool. It's the glue that bonds brand development and performance enhancement at a granular level across every marketing channel. Put simply, the more astute you become with data, the more effective your marketing becomes.

There's no either-or

In short, no profitable entity can choose sides. There is no 'brand' versus 'direct' debate. Brand marketing itself can deliver customers, and direct campaigns can help build brands – ultimately, it's all part of the same team working towards shared objectives. No matter what sector you work in, a balance is required, and the work is never done. Constant manipulation and optimisation are key.

The hallowed Vans brand has just past its 50th anniversary and its longevity and success are etched in skate park folklore. This is no fluke – it has moved with the times and balanced brand credibility with localised direct marketing, relevant digital noise, and product delivery.

Vans' social and digital footprint now reaches way beyond the playground hype of yesteryear, meaning it will likely be selling footwear to excitable grommets at 100 years old.

Chapter 35

The Dark Side Of The Moon

What happens when we know nothing about our customers?

'Setec Astronomy'.

Any fans of light-hearted, star-spangled '90s thrillers will, of course, decode this anagram immediately.

It's the cypher at the heart of the 1992 Robert Redford flick Sneakers and it translates as: -

'Too Many Secrets'.

The film hinges around a device that can unlock any code, password, or network – freeing planet Earth from its authoritarian, government-controlled mantle.

Twenty-five years on, and the world seems to have turned on its head. It's not government secrets we want to unlock.

It's our own privacy we want to protect.

For those of you who aren't plugged into TOR 24/7, I'd advise you to read 'The Dark Net' by Jamie Bartlett. In his fascinating book, Bartlett explores the evolution of privacy in the internet age, and what he uncovers is truly eye opening.

Every social media savvy adult is aware that the likes of Google, Facebook, Amazon, and their ilk are not so much service providers as weapons grade data miners. Their ability to understand, target, retarget and exploit their users means that we, the consumer, are left seemingly powerless to their glittery charms. They seem to know what we want before we do – and then handily serve it through an ad or pop up with a one click PayPal link just at the instant we're ready to buy.

The social networks are particularly good at utilizing and monetizing the hidden knowledge they glean as they work out how to justify their stratospheric stock valuations. It reminds me of that wonderful quote on the blindness of the average consumer:

"If you're not paying for the product, you are the product" (Andrew Lewis AKA blue_beetle, August 2010, with a nod to Richard Serra, 1973)

This can be simplified very neatly to that well-worn poker adage: - *"If you can't see the sucker at the table, get up – because it's you"*.

It seems, however, that awareness of this happening has started to seep through to common perception. Consumers don't like being known on such an intimate level by organisations we can't put a face to.

They feel like privacy matters.

The push against this cyber intrusion started a while ago, with the inauguration of the Cypherpunk movement.

Despite sounding like a (frankly rubbish) post dystopian musical genre, Cypherpunk activists have been around since the early '90s. They're code-astute developers and social warriors who champion cryptography and privacy-defending technology to define, build and defend socio-political change.

The group's purpose was best defined in A Cypherpunk's Manifesto (Eric Hughes, 1993):

"Privacy is necessary for an open society in the electronic age... We cannot expect governments, corporations, or other large, faceless organizations to grant us privacy ... We must defend our own privacy if we expect to have any. ... Cypherpunks write code. We know that someone has to write software to defend privacy, and ... we're going to write it".

From small collective roots the Cypherpunk movement's influence can now be seen in every corner of the business world from cyber security to Snapchat. For example, their collective coding talent contributed towards the explosion in the Blockchain, which in turn facilitated the creation of Bitcoin.

The Blockchain is a type of distributed ledger, which is a chain of information blocks linked together by an exceptionally clever method for verifying the veracity of the data contained in the blocks. The Blockchain has no 'owner' yet it enables parties who know nothing about each other to form and maintain a consensus about a set of data. That data can be anything from votes in an election to title deeds - and the applications are endless. In effect, the technology guarantees trust.

The cornerstone of Blockchain (and the reason it's the hub on which so many popular technologies are built) is that there is no role for any corporate or government owner. This provides a potential solution for the growing fear of centralised storage of sensitive data – and also one of best ways of 'sticking it to the man'. (Gizmodo can explain the basics of Blockchain better than I ever could).

In effect, Blockchain enables trust in a world without trust.

Blockchain and its child Bitcoin have opened up a new world in which consumers are able to wrestle back their online identities – they have a means to exchange money freely in a secure, private environment.

Which means total security and integrity for any peer to peer transactions.

Which means no more payment processing charges.

Which means seamless online commerce.

Which means no VISA or Mastercard.

So why would we need banks?

It's an enthralling topic and one that fuels ten thousand Troll infested debates in forums around the world every day. If this is only one of many deliverables of a more private online universe, then total personal anonymity sounds pretty cool.

Unless you're in marketing...

We thrive on data. It's second only to Starbucks on a modern marketing professional's morning 'to do' list.

So, what will become of our predictable marketing world as we get access to increasingly smaller and less detailed pockets of customer information? How will we target them if we have no idea what they want or need to buy? What happens to programmatic as tracking and analytics become less accurate with the increased use of Tor and equivalent hidden networks?

Do we go back 30 years to big brand building strategies with TV, outdoor, radio and Billboards - fighting for an incrementally crowded ATL environment? Or is product quality, brand reputation, price, customer choice and word of mouth the future mainstays of a successful marketing strategy?

The first thing businesses and their marketing teams do when faced with a threat is to look at mitigating the risk. This very publication looked at the implications of new online ad laws and EU privacy controls in January 2017 with the consensus that they weren't as archaic as originally feared. Even the proposal to allow tracking of consumers using ad blockers was allowed through.

"Privacy activists had argued the practice was illegal, but the EU now says that is not the case". (Sarah Vizard, MW, Jan 2017).

According to the same article, ISBA welcomed the move, stating that banning ad blocking software "...put the internet funding model under threat" and that the reforms were "...broadly advertiser friendly".

So far, so good right?

Wrong.

Consumers don't give a flying hoot if ad blocking isn't friendly to advertisers. It's about as high on their priority list as sourcing an especially virulent verruca or bath time with George Galloway. They're equally dismissive of data mining, with over 82% of consumers surveyed by KPMG in 2016 "...not comfortable with the sale of their data to third-parties".

There are many and varied ways in which a consumer can avoid the virtual drones that behaviourally track and data mine their habits online. For starters, go and have a look at The Onion Router – commonly known as TOR (on second thoughts, read the next three paragraphs before you do...)

The Deep Web (or Darknet– choose your preferred sobriquet) is where people – anyone – can browse literally anything without threat of observation. And yes, that means things get murky down there pretty fast. My personal favourite (and most accurate) advice for newbies to the TOR network is from a chap called 'Joe' on Yahoo answers back in 2013: -

"Don't get me wrong, there are some good things there (Lots of information, freedom of speech in foreign countries, etc.) but for the most part, only bad things are there. To sum it up, it is for the most part a collection of everything wrong with the world today..."

"Once again, I repeat DO NOT GO THERE! I am not joking when I say only bad things will come of it".

So... *this* is the fluffy utopia where the likes of you and I need to go in order to avoid the prying eyes of governments, giant corporates, social networks, ad servers and tracking software.

Super.

Intrigue piqued; I obviously went down there to have a look around myself. Unfortunately, Joe was absolutely spot on in his appraisal – it does resemble the seventh circle of hell in the Dark Net. Add to that a binge read of Mein Kampf, a lifetime watching interpretive French Mime and bumping into a lascivious Katie Hopkins on her hands and knees and you're not even close to the horror. It was a proper rummage round the hurt locker and honestly, it's best left alone.

What the existence of TOR does demonstrate in abundance, however, is that the technology is widely available and amply used to duck under the radar if you so wish. The Cypherpunk movement (amongst others) are making significant inroads (through the likes of Bitcoin) into new networks, products, and technologies to hide the identity and behaviour of individuals without the murk that exists in the current Deep Web's crevices.

If we twin that technological capability with the obvious consumer desire for invisibility, we're apparently moving towards a 'dark market' in which brands will have to sell blindly and consumers will cherry pick what they want or need with few of the external influences that marketers currently hurl at them.

In a more 'real' and less sinister world, brands will recognize the threat for what it is – consumers resetting the equilibrium and using the technology available to them to protect their personal interests and intentions thus enhancing their ability to choose freely.

Cryptography and code used against the overlords. Rage against the machine.

It's worth remembering that human beings have had integrated ad blockers installed since the dawn of man – they're called eyelids. A few billion people every day voraciously and actively devour communication and messaging through the things they read and watch and ignore things that bore them – like adverts.

Not wanting to harp on about the buzz words of the decade 'engagement' and 'content' but giving people a sales message in a format they actually enjoy is already employed with huge success by the likes of Red Bull, Lego, and Dollar Shave Club. Then there's the 'half 'n half's' – content partnerships twinning brands with appropriate entities that make things consumers seek out in their millions – see Samsung and Casey Neistat as a prime example of the genre.

What you're hunting for is active eyeballs and a smile of recognition, not a covert game of hide and seek.

I suspect that the brands that'll win their hearts and minds in the Dark Market future are those sympathetic to popular desires. The ones that focus their efforts on the '4 P's' of product, price, place, and promotion. If the options available for brands are to fight against public perception and desire or simplify their approach to focus on customer needs and wants, I'd back the latter option every time.

That said, we live in a competitive world fuelled with increasing vigour by money and growth, which means it's unlikely every business will be happy to soften their approach, relax their aggressive desire to sell and become collaborative in their communications relationship with their consumers.

The desire to maintain visibility on the public's behaviour goes all the way to the top. Only recently, two Stanford researchers working on public key cryptography (codes the government wouldn't be able to crack) received a letter from a government agency. If they openly discussed their findings it would be deemed equivalent to exporting nuclear arms to a foreign power (Tim Harford, BBC News, April 2017). In the early Cypherpunk days of Usenet and BBS (bulletin board system) the U.S. authorities were blocked from monitoring some of the less salubrious newsgroups, so they resorted to the 'tried and tested' method of bugging those under investigation. Perhaps brands of the future could follow suit? Keep tabs on consumer behaviour in their homes and cars? Bug the fridge, perhaps?

Yep, sadly we're way past that Blade Runner apocalypse already. The Internet of Things really isn't as cosy as it sounds and A.I. devices from Apple, Microsoft, Samsung, and Amazon (plus many car manufacturers) are already well ahead of the lifestyle monitoring curve.

There's an ever-widening chasm between commerce and consumer – and it's up to us as marketers to act as the bridge between the two before they irrevocably divorce.

The customer has spoken, and right now they feel like 'captive martyrs'.

Chapter 36

It's The Beginning Of The End Of The Travel Industry's Golden Age

Virgin Atlantic filing for chapter 15 bankruptcy protection in 2020 might have signalled a turning point in how we travel – and how airline brands make money.

Like many others, I spent much of the first Covid Lockdown waiting to hear back from an airline, having had flights cancelled. After enduring an overly onerous process to claim a refund, British Airways (BA) stoically announced that instead of my money, they'd be sending me some travel vouchers "in due course".

"But I asked for a refund," I answered, somewhat surprised.

"Tough. We're keeping your money and offering you and your family the chance to fly at some undefined point in the future whether you want to or not," they didn't reply, but the gist was the same.

A browse of social media and various consumer rights forums showed that BA wasn't alone among airlines in keeping hold of travellers' cash. Now, with news that Virgin Atlantic has filed for chapter 15 bankruptcy protection in New York and initiated proceedings in the high court in London, that desire to hoard the loot seems more understandable.

As with Virgin Australia, which went into administration in April owing A$6.8bn (£3.7bn) to 12,000 creditors before agreeing to be bought by Bain Capital, a Virgin Atlantic pilot tells me this is more about recapitalising the airline than going out of business. Nevertheless, the International Air Transport Association (IATA) was quoted as early as May as saying that airline losses from the pandemic could reach billions of dollars globally. At the same time, the aviation consultancy CAPA predicted that "most airlines in the world will be bankrupt" without help.

Numerous airlines worldwide have now stopped flying for good, including the UK's Flybe. Despite efforts from the government and, ironically, Virgin Atlantic, the regional airline entered administration in March and subsequently ceased operations.

Beyond the pandemic, nobody knows which airlines have the cash (or, more likely, the debt facility) to survive and latterly thrive. What is unquestionable is that air travel as we knew it is over. In an interview with Harvard Business Review (HBR) in May, Jon Ostrower, editor-in-chief of aviation publication The Air Current, was asked how passenger experience of international air travel would likely change post-pandemic.

"I suspect flying may become more boring for a while, as airlines try to recover financially. We've already seen airlines pulling in-flight entertainment systems... There will be huge pressures on the cost side."

Cost savings won't be the only item on the agenda for change. As margins tighten, the need to maximise profitability will increase, meaning empty seats simply won't be abided. Wide-bodied jets will likely fall out of favour in preference for more nimble, regional aircraft that can be filled more easily.

Additionally, business travel will likely become more restricted as CFOs push for more video conferencing in place of costly international trips. The 'Zoom boom' has been one of the few positives to come out of lockdown, but unfortunately for airlines, the posh seats are the ones they would really like to keep full. This excellent 2017 video report by Wendover Productions on the economics of long-haul airline seating demonstrates the potential value of different seat classes, illustrated with the handy infographic below.

Potential revenue from plane seat classes based on 100% occupancy at full price – more expensive seats on the right

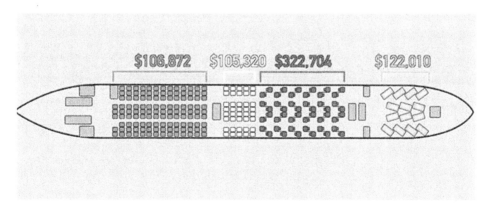

(Source: Wendover Productions, 2017)

The example looks at a British Airways 777 round-trip, non-stop flight between London and Washington, DC. The front sections of the plane account for 45% of the seats but, at full price, represent 84% of the potential revenue when fully occupied (though they usually aren't).

For us laypeople in cattle class, we're dead-headers – making up the numbers to pay for airplane fuel, while those who turn left are relied upon for profit. For anyone else over 5ft 11in who has flown intercontinentally in an economy seat recently, the idea that we don't really matter to airlines won't come as any great surprise. And yet it's the premium, business and first-class seats that are most likely to be replaced by a webcam and a Zoom/Hangouts/Teams account.

When it comes to the short-haul airlines, easyJet, Wizz Air and everyone's least favourite airline Ryanair have all pounced upon the softening of lockdown, adding flights, and aggressively pushing flash sales to get full planes airborne again. While their smaller planes are easier to fill than their long-haul siblings, there's no doubt these firms are fearful for their uncertain future, with panic-selling sales being the first iteration of their attempts at recovery.

In times of crisis and change, there are always fast-moving predators who can manipulate a market – bucking trends and turning poo into profit. In his HBR interview, Ostrower was asked who the winners would be from the slowdown in the aviation industry.

"Amazon. Surprise, surprise! As airlines retire their wide-body aircraft and shrink their fleet, the aircraft are going to conversion shops to become cargo planes and then sold to companies like Amazon. The glut of aircraft is going to drive the price down."

Despite a historically strong brand and customer advocacy, even national carriers like BA aren't immune to the current crisis. IATA has stated that airlines won't recover any sooner than 2024, if they do at all. In the meantime, those stuck in the UK could do worse than exploring the hundreds of thousands of less popular holiday destinations outside south-west England, thus doing your bit for the planet's CO_2 emissions and also to aid the recovery of beleaguered B&Bs, holiday parks, pubs and restaurants that are in as much trouble as the airlines.

Sadly for them, these business owners have significantly less chance of a bailout, and they're well aware of John Paul Getty's famous take on their situation: "If you owe the bank $100 that's your problem. If you owe the bank $100m, that's the bank's problem."

As with all other industries, those travel brands that innovate to offer the best solutions and prices for customer needs and have the flexibility and speed to move on opportunities quickly, will fly out of Covid-19 with confidence. Others will join Virgin Atlantic in the courts, simply trying to keep their engines ticking over.

Chapter 37

What If God Was One Of Us?

The vital importance of ethical and responsible marketing

If you've made it this far in the book and you're still eager to develop your marketing career, then great! Amazing! I couldn't be happier for you! But here's the caveat - in your marketing career, you'll be asked to do some grimy shit that sways deep into unethical territory. When there's big money involved, or when things aren't going so well, ethics and morality can be the most disposable of redeeming traits for some people.

You don't have to follow them down this path. In fact, doing the right thing as opposed to the most profitable thing is often the key to your customer's hearts in the long term...

Had it (or they) existed, Adam and Eve would have had no real use for a new 64Gb iPhone X with double data package. If they wanted to explore, they could walk around the limitless bounds of Eden at will with no need to plug into Waze. Dating was a foregone conclusion, no formal employment meant no email and if they wanted to chat, they could simply talk to each other.

The apple that did have a certain allure was literal, yet totally forbidden. That was until a wily snake, oozing sales savvy from every scale, used all the direct marketing tricks in the book, from brand hype to negging, in order to close the aspirational Eve. In a trick mimicked by Millennialhungry brands to this day, he suggested parental disapproval to entice and excite the naïve Eve even more.

He then sweetened the pot with a 'buy now, pay later' sales promotion device.

Behaviour like this and the subsequent fall out for every human being on the planet (granted, there were only two of them) set a nasty precedent for dirty marketing tricks and nefarious sales tactics. Cain and Able looked like a prime case for no win, no fee litigation. Noah instigated the early equivalent of a Sandal's couple's holiday ("Cruise with me – or sink to your untimely death" – classic Noah) and Lot's wife just had to look in the right place to win a lifetime's supply of salt.

Apparently, God found all this Gung Ho marketing activity more than a little trying, so in a rather grandiose statement He sent a list of guidelines down to Moses via Mount Sinai, carved in tablets rather than the more user friendly native App format.

By all accounts, this happened a while back now so how relevant are these rules to the modern-day marketer? Can they be salvaged, refreshed, and updated or are they as out-dated as Jesus sandals?

It seems that with the constant innovation in communications, platforms, media, and tools we've rather outgrown His early efforts and have ridden roughshod over the 10 Commandments in order to make a buck.

1. 'You shall have no other gods before Me' has been wholeheartedly ignored, at least if 4,200+ alternate religions and Bieber's Insta channel are to be believed.
2. "You shall not make idols". Pop, American, Indian, New Zealand –

there are now over 46 variants around the world with versions broadcast to more than 6.6 billion people in 150 countries. Take that, Commandment 2!

3. "You shall not take the name of the LORD your God in vain". Joel Scott Osteen, known as 'Pastor Joe' to his 20 million monthly viewers in over 100 countries is an extraordinary salesman trading under the catchy job title of 'Televangelist'. Go and have a gander on YouTube – if this guy's grip on the scriptures were any looser, he'd spill the bulk of the $60 million he reportedly scammed (sorry, raised) from his adoring flock. Jesus wept, and God would probably go a step further.

4. "Remember the Sabbath day, to keep it holy". A tricky one to defend, Commandment number 4, because Sainsbury's and friends being open on a Sunday is actually pretty useful to most of us.

5. "Honor your father and your mother". It still amazes me that I'm bombarded with TV ads for car insurance, supermarkets, loo roll, new sparkly Smartphones and a seemingly endless line in things that look like butter (but surely can't be butter) and yet a demographic of nearly 12 million over 65's (ONS, July 2017) remain woefully under-served. Many of them time rich and cash wealthy thanks to booming property values, we should perhaps add an addendum to this Commandment: - 'Also, remember the grandparents'.

6. 'You shall not murder'– Exhibit A – Kendall Jenner for Pepsi. Death by a thousand cuts. Think, you high-spending, sugar-rushing numpties – think!

7. 'You shall not commit adultery'. We can put at least some of the blame for breaking this one on the shoulders of the consumer – they're a fickle bunch, for sure. However, their reasons to chop and change at

the first sight of a BOGOF deal is simply the market responding to value urges above brand advocacy. Loyalty has to be earned – repeatedly, it seems. Brand switching is an unfortunate side effect of working in a vibrant economy so you can either cut your cost, improve product quality, or sprinkle magic fairy dust on your brand to make it hyper desirable.

8. 'You shall not steal'. Have you seen an original ad this year? Like the movie industry relying on sequels, it looks like we're in serious danger of running out of new ideas. As a regular TV watcher and semi-professional procrastinator, the frequency with which I get déjà vu is getting quite galling and plagiarism is rife. A cursory glance at Private Eye's 'Ad Nauseam' column last week flags up such esteemed perpetrators as Nestle/ JWT with a secondhand KitKat ad and the BBC/ Y&R with their Winter Olympics campaign.

    I'd love to be a fly on the wall in some of these client presentations, applauding a strutting ECD with recycled You Tube idea in one hand and a five zeros invoice in the other.

9. 'You shall not bear false witness against your neighbor'. This one means don't lie, doesn't it? Well white lies in marketing are fine, I assume, otherwise we're really going to have to start from scratch with 'Honesty'. However, this may not be such a bad thing, as fans of Dudley Moore's 1990 classic movie Crazy People will attest.

10. 'You shall not covet your neighbour's wife'. This Commandment is particularly topical. In late January 2018 reports seeped through Vice and Motherboard about 'Fake App' – a tool that can overlay someone's face onto a video body. Like your colleague's face onto Jabba the Hut's slithering form. Or a young Hollywood starlet into a

porn film, thus facilitating a billion illegitimate, illegal, phony sex tapes. It's disgusting, deplorable and deserves to be banned for the rest of eternity. I'm kind of surprised none of the popular gods have had a word with the App's makers (/r/deepfakes if anyone wants to let him know their feelings on the matter).

These days, the ASA, CAP Codes, CIM, GDPR & Ofcom (See Glossary ad infinitum...) are the core regulatory bodies for UK marketing, advertising, PR & TV professionals. Higher risk product categories like food, alcohol, beauty products, environmentally friendly products, medicines, tobacco, and gambling have supplemental sub-sets of guidelines, in some cases added voluntarily on top of those. Additionally, many are introducing proactive communications guidelines to protect their ability to market themselves in the future. However there remain some significant gaps - some practical, some ethical and some just common sense.

As consumers have become increasingly savvy and choices available to them broader, it seems there would be considerable benefit in updating our own advertising and marketing industry Commandments beyond the letter of the law. Acting right (as opposed to simply following the guidelines to the least viable extent) would show a responsible, customer-centric intent and a long-game view that intense competition and the hunger for success appear to have shunted firmly to the sidelines.

Having completed a seven-day turnaround on creation the Earth, the universe and everything, God apparently "...saw all that he had made, and it was very good".

Perhaps it's time to draw up a set of your own Commandments – a personal check list of how you can act more responsibly in your marketing - and maybe you'll be able to say the same.

Epilogue

It could have been worse – so now, you can make it better.

In early January 2021, in the midst of lockdown, my dad had a stroke.

After parenthood, running your own business and a shitty lockdown year, you imagine you're battle ready for anything.

Turns out, I wasn't.

My mum rang me, mid-morning on the day in question – she was as stoic as ever giving the news, albeit scared as hell. He'd felt strange after breakfast, laid down on the sofa, asked my mum, oddly, to itch his feet (a cerebral hangover of some strokes, apparently) – the medical descriptor is worded far better than anything I could craft:-

"Neuropathic itch is a potent trigger of reflex and volitional scratching although this provides only fleeting relief".

Within a crucially efficient half an hour (thanks – again - to the NHS), he was on route to the best stroke clinic in the land at the Royal Berks Hospital in Reading where, coincidentally, I'd arrived on this planet forty-three years earlier.

After a nightmarish few days with emergency surgery on (then off) the cards, he was allowed home. His speech was slow but motility, sentient thought and humour were intact. A lucky escape, in stroke terms.

He was latterly taken in for the necessary carotid artery surgery at the John Radcliffe Hospital in Oxford (I won't breach his privacy with the details, but Christ, it sounded gritty) and, after not an insignificant number of hours, regained consciousness with his speech, movement, and marbles intact.

So why should you care? This is the conclusion to a book offering advice and guidance about the marketing industry. Why the hell are you reading about the author's sick father?

Here's why:

Things have been shit, life is short, and I feel a dose of brutal honesty would be a refreshing change from the normal self-serving, hubristic, 'holier-than-thou' bullshit that usually wraps up business books like this.

'Shape your future', 'Imagine your success', 'Own your destiny', 'Define your purpose', 'Carpe Diem' - that kind of guff might sound inspiring and may even look good at the end of Nike ad, but for an aspiring young marketer, motivating buzz-speak is about as useful as Boris Johnson's hairbrush – and in real life would be used equally infrequently.

I don't know about you. I don't know who you are. I strongly suspect that some readers were just drawn in by the click-baity title.

Most people who produce content for books like this fall into one or more of the following categories:

A love of writing, link building for SEO benefit, building a personal/ business profile, sharing some deep-seated marketing/ brand/ digital/ data/ agency beliefs, selling something, PR, and ego. (There do seem to be some holistic teachers out there who write to educate their readers, but they're in the minority).

I usually don't get paid to write – few do. But I enjoy writing, and there's a loose understanding that the trade magazines I write for get legible, non-puff-piecey content in exchange for me getting self-promotion, a minor uplift in marketing kudos and some more followers on Linked In. A bit of personal branding tied to a creative outlet. Maybe a sniff of interest from a bored Head-hunter one day.

This is what I wanted to discuss. A bit of balls to the floor honesty. Something *seriously* lacking in the marketing industry. Which comes down to one unwritten but irredeemable truth:

We lie for a living.

There's no equivocation - we do. Every day, internally and externally, whether we have to or not. Our white lies, partial truths, creative interpretations and massaging of facts are as habitual as our morning Latte. Client side or agency, you're either strategizing and briefing the lies or storyboarding, writing, and campaigning the lies. It doesn't matter – I'm not judging, I'm in the same waterlogged boat.

The marketing and advertising industries are littered with the corpses of lies:

- This is the best car ever
- It tastes amazing
- This will solve everything
- Safer than ever before
- Great for kids
- Cheaper and easier
- Healthy and good for you

- We're a bank that cares
- Quicker/ faster/ more
- Lose weight (the easy way)
- Make money. Fast.
- Listen to our purpose – we mean it
- Trust us…

We work in a contradiction. Of course, after even a brief moment's consideration, you all know it, too. But we, and the brands we represent, can never admit that truth in public. The emperor's new clothes would not just be invisible – they'd burst into flames.

And the marketing industry lives in fear of this very combustibility.

So, we accept our responsibility as superior intellectual guardians of the public's purchase decisions and create the trends, tides and times that reassure them about what it is that goes in their real or virtual baskets.

Everyone lives in a happy state of (nearly) blind denial.

There's no fix for this, by the way. Most of my (and my fellow columnist's) articles usually close with a pithy conclusion. Wise words outlining how it could be done better. How there's a better way to devise strategy, to operate, to educate, to have purpose, to look after the customer, to generate the kind of success only disruptive tech brands can dream of.

Much of this is bollocks. Nobody really knows.

We work hard. We try our very best. We learn as we go. We jump on and off bandwagons because people we know and trust say they're essential. We bullshit our CEOs and clients when it comes time to talk money. Some things work great, some don't. Advertising usually has some kind of positive impact, no matter how shoddy the ad. Some campaigns win awards and don't deliver against KPIs at all. Some boring campaigns keep businesses alive.

It's a conundrum. An ever changing, exciting, unnerving, and scary one.

Much like my dad's recent scare, negative things come out of the blue to turn your life on its head, and there is nothing – NOTHING – you can do about it. Apart from grit your teeth, shore up your own personal resolve and march on.

Everything else in life, as in your career, is manageable if you put it in perspective.

So, try to do work you enjoy, educate yourself whenever possible, aim high, work hard, listen, ask questions, have fun, be nice to people and make the creative and media industries a force for good, not evil.

If you do that, you won't go far wrong.

Harry Lang, November 2021

About the Author...

Harry Lang was born in Reading in England and grew up in the beautiful Berkshire village of Stanford Dingley. Having been to school at Elstree and Harrow, he spent three glorious years at Newcastle University studying Geography. Sometimes.

After a brief student internship at Saatchi & Saatchi, he graduated with a 2:1 in 1999 and entered the M&C Saatchi graduate program working in the sponsorship division as a minion for the Benson & Hedges/ Jordan Formula 1 account team.

He then started his strategic apprenticeship at Creatif Marketing Consultants in Bermondsey before joining 141 Worldwide, the integrated arm of the Bates advertising group in 2001, where he managed accounts for British American Tobacco and Allied Domecq. A brief stint at youth marketing agency Angel followed where he worked for his dream client, Penguin Books, on its multi award winning 'Are You Good Booking?' campaign.

A move back to big agency life saw him running the Budweiser account at Inferno, and he also had a hand in creating the 'Keyboard Guitar' viral campaign for Sony PlayStation. A disgruntled client saw an enforced but well-funded exit, and a joyous period of gardening leave, during which he travelled Europe and wrote his first unpublished novel, 'Parabolic'.

A planned migration to Sydney was curtailed with a job offer in an online poker start-up, Goalpoker.com. Strip club status meetings, random gangsters, a pop video and renting a 737 on a credit card to fly twenty models (and a former EastEnders cast member) to Ibiza are just the chapter headings for this disastrous/ amusing segment of his career, and the inevitable implosion of the business pushed him into a series of more stable roles in the gaming industry - from CWC Gaming's Costa Rica/ Macau adventures to the launch of Jackpot Party.com for WMS.

In 2012, Harry moved to Spain to work in Gibraltar as Head of Marketing at bwin.party after which he took another period of gardening leave and wrote his second unpublished novel, 'Try Morality'. Remaining in Southern Europe, he spent 2014 as a consultant for Mecca Bingo. He enjoyed an idyllic three years by the beach in Sotogrande and was married at the Monasterio de San Martin in 2014.

On returning to the UK with a desire to leave the gambling industry in 2015, Harry failed dismally and became Executive Marketing Director at leading sportsbook Pinnacle.com. In 2017 he founded Brand Architects as a brand a marketing consultancy and he and his wife welcomed their beloved daughter to the world in 2018.

In 2020 he joined one of his clients, Buzz Bingo, as Marketing Director and at the time of writing is on the cusp of joining tech scale up Stint.co, the leading student staffing platform in the hospitality industry, as CMO.

Harry lives in South West London and enjoys skiing, golf, cycling, rugby, writing and reading when time allows.

Endorsements for Brands, Bandwagons & Bullshit

Many thanks to these awesome individuals for their support: -

Rory Sutherland, Vice Chairman at Ogilvy, said this about 'Brands, Bandwagons & Bullshit': -

"I noticed that this book ingeniously starts with a glossary - which was recommendation enough. But it gets even better from there on. I am really enjoying this".

Danny Denhard, CMO, Marketing & Growth Coach. Founder of 'Must Reads' newsletter:-

"A gripping and no-nonsense take on the complex world of marketing and how to navigate for success. This is a passionate and actionable guide for the elite marketers of the future".

Reverend Andrew Lightbown, Rector, Winslow Benefice

"This is a book that demands to be read: professional and practical, humorous and honest. Harry Lang clearly cares not only about the industry, but the people who comprise the industry. In a very real sense, and apologies for the religious sounding language, this book is concerned with the telling of truths. It is both pastoral and prophetic. What you get with Harry is the wisdom of a seasoned professional, someone who how knows how to be themselves but with skill, someone who refuses to ride every bandwagon for short term gain, and who knows the difference between healthy manure and the pernicious stench of bullshit"

Ryan Murton, Director of Organic Acquisition, Bumble.com

"This is a must read for me. A truly reflective life example on how to succeed in this dog-eat-dog industry. I resonate with it a lot".

.

Printed in Great Britain
by Amazon